SHAW

The *Nonreligious* Guide to Dating & Being Single

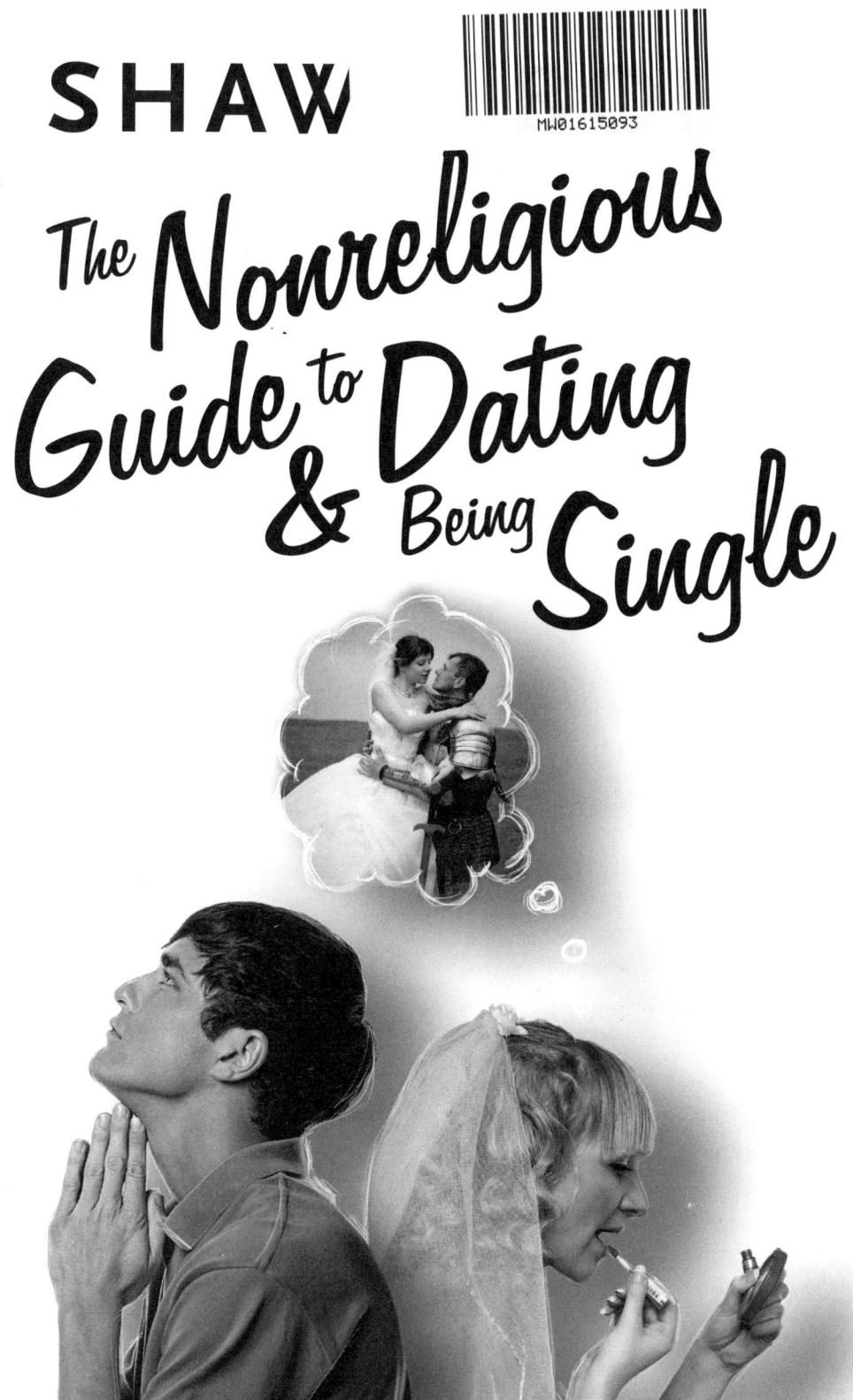

Editor: Sally Hanan—inksnatcher.com
Cover & Text Design: Dustin Bocks—dustinbocks.com

ISBN: 978-0-9822370-3-8

Dedication

I want to dedicate this book to Maximus, my Boxer dog, who cuddles with me most nights and looks deeply into my eyes to tell me that he loves me more than a wife ever could. Max, you can't, but I love you, little buddy.

Acknowledgments

This book is partly helped by my single sister, Jennifer, who is one of my closest friends and has always been an inspiration to me. Jennifer not only introduced me to Christ, she has also been one of my main examples of love and support. She loves beyond reasonable measure and cares in the deepest of ways. Whoa, I don't want to cry here so let me lighten this up. Guys, she is also still single, and I hope that all the guys who are worthy of her, and who are in an age scale of two years younger than her and ten years older than her, take notice and ask her out.

I want to thank my *MySpace* and blogging friends for helping me get this whole book started. Your feedback, support, stupidity, intelligence, irreverence, humor, kindness, and love have made this possible. The hundreds of thousands of visits to my dating blog posts showed me I needed to extend my dating advice and put it all in a book. This book is a result of your hunger!

P.S. I also want to thank every girl who has ever stalked me—for helping me to set my standards way higher than they already were.

Contents

Introduction

Well, I was going to name this *Shawn's Kick-Butt Guide to Dating and Being Single* but that would have offended some people, so I renamed it. Of course, those same people just read this introduction and are appalled and have probably stopped reading. Wow! Now I realize I could have named it that anyway! Well, let's call it that from this page forth! Welcome to *Shawn's Kick-Butt Guide to Dating and Being Single!*

Not all of this book will be written with this incredible wit or sarcasm; we do have to get serious sometimes, but in the same token, let's have fun with a subject that is always too stiff when talked about under the umbrella of Christianity.

Let me just start out by saying I am shocked I am writing this. No really, _____(insert your name here because I am talking to you, _____), I am. I never intended to address the subject of dating and relationships. I am not the hopeless romantic you can find in many a movie. I am ordinary and relatively inexperienced. Ok, ok, really inexperienced—at the time of writing this, I am in my thirties and not married, but for good reason (you will find out if you are brave enough to read on).

I think being single, and having only had a few real relationships in my life, has given me compassion for other singles. I have witnessed most (almost all) of my friends walk through relationships, and most of them are now married. I have officiated and been in weddings too many times to count, and I'm even at the point of kind of not liking the wedding scene anymore because of it (unless the person is so close I can't help but be sentimental). I have also seen dysfunction, divorce, and terrible breakups wreck people's faith in the possibility of finding true, lasting relationships. As a person looked to for different types of counsel, this is one subject the whole world seems to be asking about.

One day I received an e-mail invitation to speak at a singles' conference. I was sitting pondering why I would never do that when I got a call from a friend. She was in a very awkward relationship with many strange dynamics disturbing it. I had to have an opinion, for the sake of her very sanity.

First rule, guys, when addressing a member of the opposite gender: Don't ever have an opinion you don't want to spend some time developing. Our conversation went on longer than I had ever spent on the phone, and I was sure that if cell phones really did produce tumors, I was well on my way to receiving one. What was amazing, though, is my friend did not have a moral and romantic compass to guide her new relationship. Instead, she had religion and structure given to her by people who hadn't dated in a million years, if at all.

When you ask for advice on how to find the right one, there is nothing better (being sarcastic) than a woman saying, "Just pray!" . . . and then you find out her story: She instantly knew, through prayer, whom she was going to marry; she was pursued by him the next day, and she got married six months later without experiencing any trials in the relationship. There is an overabundance of advice being offered Christians, and it may even have a good heart behind it, but that doesn't mean it is valuable advice. All of us are completely different. Look around! You will notice no one with the same makeup as you.

So here is the question: How do you set good boundaries for yourself by using the wisdom of others without being limited by their experiences? If you are legalistic, it means you do everything in your life according to rules someone else wrote or taught you. You let their rules tell you how you should think. Legalistic rules violate relationships because they become more important than love. If every relationship is different, how do you follow your heart in a way that you can still protect it without being a rule follower or a legalistic person?

I want to be careful writing this book because it's not meant to be one more "five easy steps to get into relationship" or "if you do the following five things in a relationship you will destroy it." This book is not an exhaustive manuscript on the subject of being single, dating, and/or relationships; instead, it is more of a project to challenge your way of thinking and to help you put the right boundaries in place for you. It is a philosophical document which explores our changing culture and our role in it.

There are books which can help you define what you want in a relationship, teach you how to pray relationships in, kiss relationships goodbye, and that sort of thing. This book does more than that because it makes fun of many of those books without my even trying!

Many of them were written with a very self-focused Christian or cultural view that may not translate well to all of society; it's like taking the principles from an Amish social and applying them to your next dinner party. The principles work well in the small Amish-type community (aka a Christian subculture), but I dare you to do an Amish costume party in Hollywood—it will feel like a bad sarcastic joke! My goal is to provide the opposite of a very marginalized book, and I hope you will have a much freer way of thinking about dating after reading it.

For all of those single people who are on the road to balanced relationships (and are sick of the extremes in both the world and the church), for parents, and even those already in a relationship, this is your time. This is your book!

Shawn

P.S. I consider it a great privilege to speak into the relational process because God loves relationships. They can be the most beautiful and painful things in our lives. At the same time, I do want to qualify that I do not do: singles' conferences, premarital or marital counseling (at least I try not to) and, dating seminars, nor do I give dating advice to people I am not in relationship with. This book is one of my only efforts to speak into this subject (outside of my own relational structure).

P.P.S. I have some disclaimers to make on this book.

Disclaimer #1: Nothing written in here is meant to be controversial or offensive. This book is not a theology book, it's a philosophical and entertaining book; therefore, do not stop reading just because you don't agree with one point. It is a book that presents a series of values which will help you set standards for your own relationships. Even if you do not agree with one of the values, you may be helped by others. There are so many church cultures and backgrounds, even in the US alone, that some of the things I say are obviously going to be different than the theological and philosophical input of others. The good thing about reading another's perspective, even if it is not entirely complimentary to yours, is it helps sharpen what you personally believe.

If the content of this book stirs up a reaction in you, you are welcome to visit my *MySpace* (where the blog posts were originally done on this subject) or my book's fan page on Facebook and rant at me or cry or hate me or love me or encourage me via the comments box.

Disclaimer #2: I am writing this book for adults, not for youth. It can be helpful for youth, but I believe youth need their parents to help set personal boundaries and a moral compass from within. It's different for adults. I am not limiting youth, but I am qualifying the audience this book is intended for. There are talks of boobies and penises that make this book PG-13. The book will probably come across very differently to a mom reading it to her 15-year-old daughter (who she is trying to set values with) than to a mom of maybe that same girl at 29 who is not married.

Disclaimer #3: While there are some awesome books on dating and relationships in the Christian world, there are also some especially ridiculous ones which have caught the conservative crowd up in a storm of dating bureaucracy that kills true passion. I do want to point out I am not singling out any books for criticism, or making fun of others. We need a variety of sources on the subject of dating, and each one probably brings its own measure of truth . . . even if it is not as much fun as this one.

Living Outrageously Single!

Living Outrageously Single, & Other Single Clichés

So let's start by talking about sex. Oh wait, that subject comes later, and what a great subject it is! Let's not pause for a moment here to think about it, because I need you to be in a spiritual frame of mind. No really, please come back to the page . . . look down at the words . . . there you are. Welcome back!

Before we talk about anything else, we need to establish a foundation. This is the headiest part of the book, but stay with me; it's worth it. Let me make a statement right off the bat which is important:

If you are a Christian, you do not have to be married, but you can choose to be.

If you are consumed with the need to be married, then you are not living in the simplicity of Christianity which Jesus paid a huge price for you to walk in. Let me show you what I mean. It all has to do with God's desire for you.

Need vs. grace

I would define the relationship Adam and Eve had with one another before the fall as being a desire to share enjoyment with another being. It was the same desire which caused God to create man in the first place: He wanted man to enjoy His company and everything He had made. Even though Adam and Eve were joined to each other by God, they had intimacy with Him first. They were united with God in a special love that had no earthly comparison. The enjoyment of their union with God played out in their union and relationship with each other—it was their choice and desire to share themselves with each other.

When Adam and Eve were sent out of the garden, one of the consequences was the fact that their fellowship with God was broken and, because of it, the dynamics of their relationship changed. They were separated from God and bound to each other (Genesis 3:17–18). The desire to share fellowship and intimacy with each other changed from a choice to a need or a dependency on each other. Fellowship with each other could not be chosen out of an emotional and mental place of total freedom anymore because God was not as present in the relationship.

Jesus' prayer

The cultural trend in the Old Testament was that people (for the most part) would get married and work a normal job or raise kids, and that was their lot and their only hope for fulfilling their purpose in life. They didn't know it, but Old Testament marriage was a redemptive picture of God's covenant desire to share Himself with His people and to show them what eternity would be like.

Jesus drove home this desire when He prayed:

> "I do not ask for these (followers) only, but also for those who will believe in me through their word, that they may all be one, just as you, Father, are in me, and I in you, that they also may be in us . . . The glory that you have given me I have given to them, that they may be one even as we are one, I in them and you in me, that they may become perfectly one" (John 17: 20-23).

When Jesus prayed to have union with us, He was praying for the original plan of heaven to be reestablished on earth. The Father honored His desire and, because of redemption, we can be one with Jesus. The Holy Spirit has restored us to a place of unity with Him.

We have our longing for deep relationship fulfilled through the Holy Spirit! He is the fulfillment of that desire! This is His grace. Though we need relationships, we don't necessarily need an earthly counterpart to have a fulfilled life on earth. This doesn't mean we will not have to work on our relationship with the Holy Spirit. In some ways, this spiritual relationship can hold less immediate gratification than an earthly one; but when we pursue God with a whole heart, we get to live through, and have, the eternally true and fulfilling unity with Him that Jesus prayed (and died) for.

Marriage in the New Testament

One of the most powerful demonstrations of the fact marriage may not be important to your fullness of life is that spouses are rarely ever mentioned in the New Testament. None of the apostles had a recorded wife except Peter. Martha and Mary had no recorded marriages either. The list of those who remained unmarried goes on. While the New Testament doesn't discount marriage, it does invalidate it as a primary need of a Christian's humanity. This can either confuse us or encourage us about how awesome an intimate spiritual journey with Jesus can be. The New Testament helps us to refocus our desires by placing them first on Jesus and secondly on other God-given relationships such as marriage.

Paul saw we could find fulfillment in life without marriage. He taught marriage as neither an obligation nor a sin. He contrasted marriage against the single life (1 Corinthians 7:31–35), and he ended his contrast by saying, "I am sharing this for your own good, not to restrict you, but that you may live in a right way, in undivided devotion to the Lord." Paul encouraged virgins to remain unmarried (1 Cor. 7:8) because in our fellowship with Jesus, through the Holy Spirit, we are bound by a new covenant of fellowship with God. Being married does not have to be the central part of it. Of course, I can listen to Paul's advice, but I am still free to make my own choice about getting married some day. See? In my own life, my soul (mind, will, and emotions) is even more powerful than Paul's. I have to follow my heart.

For those who do not have Christ, marriage is the highest place of relational fulfillment they can achieve because of God's blessing on marriage, but they are still bound to each other by need and dependency. We, though, are no longer bound to Adam and Eve's state of being, which basically mandates us to be married because it is a need in our lives. We can have true relationship with the Trinity and the friendship of the body, letting those relationships meet our primary needs for unity. Marriage is an additional opportunity, blessing, or choice.

Because of Christ, you can be outrageously single

In this book, I am not calling married people spiritually inferior. Marriage is one of the purest pictures of what a believer can have when in union with Jesus. At the same time, marriage is not the only way into this union. As a matter of fact, the closer we get to the last days, the harder it will be to stay married because of the particular challenges it will hold. Ultimately, this message is *not* anti-marriage, but it is giving room for singleness. I respect what Paul says in 1 Corinthians 7, where he warns us about false teachings which say marriage is wrong.

The whole identity of people in every culture on earth (except, possibly, where I live—in Los Angeles, where many marry their careers) is based on the idea we are not complete until we have a mate. This is true of nearly all earthbound creatures. The Bible is very clear in the New Testament, though, that Jesus completes us and we do not need anyone else but Him. The trend in teaching in the Church has always been that we have perfect matches out there for us, and that our lives will truly start when we find our mate! To make matters worse, there is an unspoken assumption in many religious structures that adulthood and true maturity only start when we get hitched. Maybe that's why I still like video games . . . I'm not married.

My point is: let's put marriage in perspective. Let's recognize we do not have a need for it to define who we are in God. God took all needs away from us and replaced them with choice. We are no longer bound by need and dependency because God fulfills us in every way. This realization actually makes marriage to a Christian more beautiful, because when we have a choice about whether to get married or not and we still choose to, it brings a greater depth of meaning to the relationship. When looked at under this light, choosing to marry someone is a picture of God's love and His desire for us. Is God not self-sufficient? Yes, God does not have a need for us, but He does have a sincere desire to share Himself with us, and this is why we were created. If we have God, do we really need anything else? We are already complete in God when we have His Spirit dwelling within us.

If you want to join in marriage to another individual because you want to:

- ☐ Enjoy someone, and share enjoyment with someone
- ☐ Truly learn about life with/from someone
- ☐ Be a picture of God's love to someone
- ☐ Do life with your best friend

then you have the right desire for marriage. If you have a sincere desire to be married for the right motivations, then by all means you should give yourself to it! But if you have a burning need in your life to just get your desires fulfilled by another person, stop! You need to find completion in God, first, because He is the source of fulfilled desires.

Freedom

You can't decide you have to be married out of loneliness. You can't have a selfish desire for marriage or it most likely will not work or will keep you stuck. As a Christian, you cannot serve two masters, and if you marry out of need, then you will have to serve this need. A house divided against itself can't stand (Mark 3:25). Serving your need in place of being fulfilled by God will eventually take your focus off God and put it on yourself, or on this other person.

Now then, not only is your life not limited by the fact you are unmarried, but there is freedom to choose whether or not to be married. This is exciting because it makes the prospect of finding a mate an adventure instead of an obsession. If you go on an adventure of marriage, it should enhance what you are already getting out of life, and should also enhance the quality of life your possible future spouse is currently living as well.

God chooses to love you, and one of the beauties of marriage is the fact that God has allowed you to choose it. If you choose to be single, you can accomplish every purpose you set for your life. If you choose to be married, then you will commit to love someone in such a way that your purposes in life will look different. Either direction is good as long as you don't live under the religiousness of obligation, and as long as love for Jesus (not a person) is your first goal.

For the record, I do have a desire to get married, but I am also happy being single—if I am single or married, I am on a journey of joy and fulfillment—in life and forever.

I'm Not Married & So Can You Be!

One of the most common questions I get asked by mothers is (picture an older Jewish mother asking this),

"Why are you not married yet?"

Some ask as if there is something wrong with me, some ask as if there is something wrong with the women in my life for not catching me yet, and some even wonder if I am gay. Can't a guy catch a break??

To build credibility with the mothers (reading this) who are constantly trying to fix me up with their daughters, nieces, sisters, and even themselves: let me take you on my journey. Oh, wait! If you take that previous line as arrogant, then you might think I am under the assumption I am an amazing catch. To be honest, I am only sought after by so many mothers and their relatives because I am in the public eye. I have no delusions of awesomeness (I say with a big grin on my face), although I do think I have a great smile and a great sense of value for myself.

My story

I never thought I would write this into a book, but sometimes someone else's journey helps you have faith for your own.

When I was twenty, I was involved with a girl who I thought I would be with forever. I had our whole life planned out, down to the names for our children. I was convinced I was going to marry this beautiful girl, and I knew she cared deeply for me as well. Then (abbreviated version) God asked me, very clearly, to walk with Him for a specific time frame of my life in a more dedicated way. I was to focus all of that period of time on Him so He could develop me further. There was nothing wrong with my love for the girl; Jesus was not punishing me. I also don't believe He only wanted to work on my character so I could be "ready" for her or someone else. He was just inviting me into a walk with Him which was special and set apart. I had a choice, and so I promised Him, "If you will fulfill my desires and keep me from deep loneliness, then I will walk with you."

I specifically felt I was not to be in a relationship during my twenties. I didn't have a cultish mind-set about it. I knew God had given me an invitation rather than a command, so I was willing to take things day by day and walk with Him as a single man. I wasn't crippled by the restraint; instead, I walked in a greater level of freedom because I didn't have to think about a spouse—who she might be and what our life might be like. I was able to focus completely on Him and my opportunities in life.

It was a choice that brought me on adventures—the like of which you wouldn't believe! Being so focused on God enabled me to go on over a thousand trips all over the world; it brought me to write several books, make tons of TV appearances, work in the video game industry, help plant the International House of Prayer in Kansas City (IHOP–KC), plant several other ministries, and connect and minister to leaders in every sphere of society. I had a single focus, time, and extra finances—all of which allowed me to become a high achiever while still enjoying life in a non-workaholic way.

I am so glad I made the deeply personal choice to walk with Him in this way for so long. He has filled my life with opportunities I just wouldn't have been able to accomplish without the freedom of being single. Because of it, I understand what Paul was saying about staying single: you aren't as distracted compared to the daily life of parenting and marital maintenance. Of course, marriage and parenting are worth the sacrifice, but both choices are valuable.

What if?

It makes me wonder: What if a generation of single Christians was to dedicate a season to God, during which each Christian would not think about a future spouse or romance? Of course, I wouldn't expect anyone to make the commitment I did, or if they did, to do it for the length of time I have; but what would happen if we allowed ourselves to be set apart first? Some people think this is very idealistic, but actually, when it's a choice, it's very practical and grace based.

Your heart might tell you to either pursue the person you meet who seems like *The One*, or to be set apart; either way, you still have a lot to learn about yourself. The odds are you don't want to be alone. You may already feel ready to pursue someone; or you may feel lonely enough to find some-one who will, at the very least, offer basic companionship, but . . . the first step in life is not about finding a relationship. It is about you. Throughout this book, we are going to cover the foundations of relationships, but it starts with singleness.

Who are you as a single, unique individual? What is your identity? What makes you tick?

Learning about You;
The Journaling Project

"I am good enough, smart enough and, doggone it, people like me!"—Stewart Smalley

When you are on a journey of life, perhaps the first most important discovery you need to make is not who you may (or may not) marry, but who you are. Having a foundational knowledge of who you are is the key to living a fulfilled life; it is the key to being who you need to be.

Many people go into relationships without any sense of self, and so they look at their relationships to define who they are. This becomes dangerous and selfish. The other thing people do is put together their dream lists of what they want in a spouse.

"Get off your butt and work on you!"—Dr. Phil

First things first: **I think what is *more* important is putting together a dream list of what you want to see God do in you!** Let's put together your very own "best version of myself" scale you can compare yourself to. Who do you want to be? Who do you want to be for a future spouse?

I also have a journaling project for you! Get out a little notebook, fire up the iPad, or open a Word document—you are going to begin to define your identity! (Use one page for each question.)

Your name here's Kick-Butt Guide to Dating and Being Single Identity Survey

1. How would I describe my ability to love people? *(Stay simple and honest, but give a paragraph of strengths and weaknesses.)* How do I describe my ability to receive love from others? *(Again, write a paragraph of strengths and weaknesses.)*

2. What are five key words that define my core strengths? What is my personal definition of those key words?

3. What are five key words that define my core weaknesses—those things that oppose who I am called to be? What is my personal definition of each word?

4. *(This is a hard one to do without training or help, but try it.)* What areas do I feel called to that I know are essential parts of my life's mission? How would I define, in one to five sentences, what my life purpose or calling is. *(These are not things like world peace, but actual dreams/ goals that make up what you are hoping your life will influence.)*

Oh, come on, we are only halfway done. Keep going! This is going to get good!

5. What are the talents I have *(that you are developing or have developed)* that I want my relationship circle to know I make use of?

Here is one of the hardest parts. Be honest. This is for you!

6. Do I like my own looks? *Describe what you like and don't like.* What would I get done to myself if I had my own extreme makeover?

7. Do I like my own personality? What are my relational strengths that come through my personality? *(Like: I am good at making people feel at home/I am good at listening/I have a good sense of humor/I like my own jokes.)*

8. Do I like my own relational abilities? Do I like the way people relate to me?

9. If I pretend I am someone of the opposite sex who's interested in me, what might be all of the dreams he/she might have for me? How do I measure up?

This is the kind of survey that puts a mirror up to you, yourself, and him/her. What's important about answering these types of questions is that in answering them, you start knowing yourself better. Some of you may need more than a quiz, or others of you feel as if it will take a journey of a few years to really know yourself. This happens best as you get to know God and others, and you can only do that by being in relationship with them.

BFF—
Friendship with the Opposite Sex

When it comes to the subject of male and female relationships, there is a weird, unbalanced overreaction in religious circles, and an overly-sexual, societal culture in the western world, that keeps men and women from having any real level of relationship. Most of this is because religion acts without love, and it reacts to weakness with control. It addresses the one-sidedness of weakness with more one-sidedness. Religion puts rules all the way across the board to compensate for human weakness, instead of calling everyone to a higher standard of love and modeling a moral compass.

Instead of overreacting to the condition of the world which, in the religious mind's perception, only causes male-female relationships to be sexualized, we need to be the agents on earth who bring balance and health. We don't need to swing to the other end of the pendulum and get so legalistic we purge all relationships with the opposite sex out of our lives.

Under the new covenant we are all called, male and female, to the high purposes of God. This means we are called to work for the glory of God, in unity, out of true affection *for* each other and out of real relationship *with* each other. This also means there is a provision of purity and balance for Christians who commit to friendships with the opposite sex.

Paul greeted several women by name in his letters, and Jesus had best friends who were women. Jesus *understood* friendship with women. He spent one-on-one time with the Samaritan woman in John 4, and Mary and Martha were considered two of his dearest friends. The world tries to pervert those friendships by saying He might have been married to one of them, or He got one of them pregnant, but we know He had pure intentions. Not only did He call these two women His true friends, He proved it by responding to their call—when their brother Lazarus died—and explaining His heart to them. He also appeared to Mary after He was resurrected, and He spoke to her as a close friend before any of his guy friends got to see Him.

Some hard questions to bring balance

1.   Can you really be friends with someone of the opposite sex?

One of the reasons I am writing this book is because of this very thing: Most friendships do not have healthy boundaries and, to date, there is not a great distinction on what healthy boundaries in a male-female friendship should look like. Because of this, many people let their friendships cross lines because they start getting attracted to someone they know in their hearts they don't want to marry. They don't know they shouldn't entertain these attractions if they value the relationships. We should try to have relational integrity.

If you have developed a normal friendship with someone you are not attracted to, and you spend real friendship time with this person, you can always maintain your boundary of not sexualizing the friendship. Everyone, though, has to define and reinforce boundaries in friendships with the opposite sex. There may be a time you begin to feel attracted to your friend, but if you have a boundary up, you will love your friend enough to let this attraction settle down or die because you know he/she is not for you romantically. It can take time to die to emotions. As a matter of fact, your desire might flare up at an inconvenient moment for both of you, but if you truly want to keep the friendship healthy, you'll be able to let your feelings go for the sake of the rich friendship. You do not have to be ruled by your feelings.

2.   What happens when you are friends with someone of the opposite sex and he/she gets married? Is it over then?

I believe God wants us to have friendships with qualities that are destined to remain exclusive to those friendships. If you have healthy friendships with others before they are married then, most likely, the friendships should continue after they are married. True friendship is not for you to use as a substitute relationship until you get married; it is part of your life and, as such, should be able to keep moving forward no matter how much your life changes.

Two of my closest girlfriends have gotten married. Our friendships were never a substitute for marriage, so it was a natural transition for all three of us. Because of being friends with the girls, I have now inherited their husbands as friends too. They all love me, and we now have more, not fewer, friends. When you have healthy friendships with the opposite sex, they add fullness to life.

I will only have one wife, so I am only going to invest the gifts of complete companionship into one woman. That one relationship will be far more than just friendship; my friendships with females will have a very different nature than will my relationship with my wife. If she is emotionally healthy, she will understand this and not be threatened by my friendships with other women, and the same goes for with me with her guy friends.

Boundaries are the key to keeping friends as friends. Do I spend a lot of alone time with married female friends? No, but sometimes we do go out for coffee or a meal. Sometimes we do talk about deep things because I am one of their processors, but they share those things with me on a lighter level than they would with their husbands because they are mutually dependent on their husbands, whereas we are just friends. If they felt they could share with me on a deeper level than with their husbands about all things, the friendships would be unhealthy and would undermine their marriages. My friendships with them have brought even more strength to their marriages—they help them in life, just as any friendship should (and of course they help me; they are give-take relationships).

My closest female friends come with me in the package of my life, just as my male friends do. God has given us destiny and purpose together, not just friendship; that means whomever I marry will inherit a bunch of new friends, just as I will inherit hers. If she wants me to put these relationships behind me, then I'll know she is not the right person to marry *or* she has some healing or maturing to go through because she doesn't have the maturity or health to appreciate what I have built in life. If friends don't transfer into this new relationship, then it has already become independent, isolated, and self-serving. Even marriage can be selfish like this.

Some of you may be reading this and you are worried because you have no true friends to bring into your marriage. I know when you get married right out of high school or college, your friendships with the opposite sex are not always as deep. Most people do not retain deep relationships with 90 percent of the people they went to school with because the friendships were only *functional*—they were held together by the function of school. Some people who are younger find it easy to leave all their friends behind because their friends were not *life* friends but *functional* friends; however, when you develop *life* friends—friendships formed for the sake of relationship—you share life with them. Many people won't bring *functional* friends into a marriage, but they should both bring in their *life* friends and begin to enjoy their spouse's.

If your date has no friends for you to inherit, it might be a concern because it means you will have to be the relational strength for both of you. If you have no friends, it means you may not be ready for a relationship. You need to learn how to be a friend to others so that you can work on your ability to love and be loved. Loners don't always make good lovers.

3. How do you know if your friendships are healthy?

Let me note, we are not talking about the kind of friendship you pursue when you are attracted to someone and you let your heart wonder about future possibilities together. We are talking about regular friendships with people you are on teams with, work with, share life with, neighbors, etc., and you have neither hope nor desire to spend your future with them in marriage. Healthy friendships take time and love.

It is unhealthy when we only look at friendships with the opposite sex as a fill-in before marriage and we choose to invest very little into them—either before or after getting hitched. When you begin to pursue attraction or cross the line in friendship with someone, but you do not see them as someone you would want to ever marry, it's called *defrauding*! When you *defraud* others you

- Keep them from their right focus in life
- Steal them from getting married to someone else
- Selfishly use them for your own desires

You may just miss forming a friendship with your own future spouse, who might come into your life in the same season you are using someone else. One of the main ways you *defraud* a friend is when you both have some sort of attraction (mental, physical, emotional, spiritual) to each other, but one of you doesn't really see a future in the relationship. The *pretend-a-friend* says: "I just want to be friends (lovers), nothing else (please love me)." In other words, they are pretending not to have feelings but they actually do. It is a heart issue (lying to yourself) before a communication issue to say: "I am not interested in you that way, and I only ever want to be friends."

Most people don't even know what *defrauding* looks like. You *defraud* by using non-committal language which avoids closure and leaves the other person in limbo, e.g. "Right now, I just want to be friends, but who knows about the future?" or "I don't have those same feelings for you, but I'll keep an open mind!" You might also give people extremely close friendship access, to the point where they begin to allow you to meet romantic relational needs that are not for you to fulfill. Don't pretend you're not dating just because you use lots of good boundary language. If you are giving others the depth of heart that should only be reserved for romance, you are defrauding them and lying to yourself by keeping it under the license of friendship.

When I wrote this chapter as a blog post, it was one of the subjects that got floods of e-mails from women who agreed. They admitted they had found themselves pretending, even to themselves, that their motives were not romantic. A lot of self-deception can creep in when you are ashamed you even have feelings. The feelings are not evil or wrong, but the character with which you handle them will determine the outcome of your friendships. While it's great to have deep conversations, and while fake boundaries might be nice, the long-term reality is that *defrauding* him/her will hurt both of you, and it will hurt the friendship. It puts the other person in a penalty box, with you holding all the control and power in the relationship. You are saying the relationship can only go forward when you make up your mind. You are leading your friend along and this is plain SELFISH! This is one of the unhealthiest things you can do in a friendship. It not only shows a lack of integrity on your part, but it will also cause others in your community to distrust you.

If you think . . .

If you think every person who compliments you is into you, then you are fooling yourself. You will rob yourself of normal, healthy, true friendships with the opposite sex if you only look at people as potential mates (or they think you do). It is called exploitation/using people, and it usually stems from not having a father or mother's voice in your life that helped you to have good emotional boundaries. Too many guys think a girl is into them if she is nice to them. Guys, she's just being *nice*.

If you are getting close to a friend of the opposite sex, and you cannot be affectionate with him/her in a normal way without this being taken as flirtation, then there is probably either:

☐ Something wrong with you
☐ Something wrong with them and the way they give affection

If you have never had healthy relationships with the opposite sex, you may be criticizing or judging what is actually healthy about other people's relationships. You might be projecting your skewed view onto theirs. Lots of times, people who have had siblings of the opposite sex are better at defining these brotherly/sisterly interactions than those who have not grown up with someone they have had natural boundaries with.

Before you declare all your friendships are as healthy as boiled spinach in oatmeal, evaluate yourself first by asking yourself these questions:

1. Have I ever had a friend of the opposite sex I didn't look at as a potential mate?

2. Do I know how to give compliments, hugs, and say *I love you* to someone I am close to without it being flirtatious?

3. Do I know how to receive a compliment, hug, or *I love you* without it affirming a romantic side of my heart?

4. Am I prone to fantasy about normal friends?

There are many people who have such a level of brokenness that they just can't be friends without adding strings to their relationships. If you are one of these people, then you have a journey of healing to go on. Maybe once you are married you will be able to define better boundaries, but even if married, don't project this imbalance onto the relationships of those who have good boundaries.

Bringing unhealthy friendships into the marriage

Because some married people have never had a healthy friendship with a member of the opposite sex, they can delude themselves into believing the friendships they have/the friendships they want to bring into the marriage are normal. In order to avoid burdening a new marriage by including unhealthy friendships, every married person needs to ask him/her self the following types of questions about his/her friends of the opposite sex:

1. Is this someone I am attracted to? Is he/she my type? Is my friend someone who my wife/husband would be naturally threatened by if we had never been friends before?

2. Do I spend too much time with this person? Do I make my spouse spend more time with this person than he/she would want to?

3. Do I find myself processing life with this friend in a way I should do with my wife/husband, and not in the way I do with my other female/guy friends?

4. Does this friend have the feeling of being like a brother/sister to me and to the rest of my family, or am I the only one who perceives that (whereas everyone else is confused as to why I would have such a close relationship with him/her while I am married)?

5. Do I find myself using his/her perspective to defend mine to my spouse (in disagreements)?

If you have healthy friendships, it is important you don't overreact to those friends who haven't (those friends who get too serious or flirtatious). Instead, you just need to put up proper boundaries. I can't tell you the number of times women, even in a group setting, have wanted to cross the line of friendship and make the time feel more like a date. This is because they choose to loosen their hearts' boundaries and try to use me to feed their need for the feeling of more intimate closeness. When this happens I put up my very real boundaries, e.g. I just bring the subject around to something that's fun, and I include some of the other people we are hanging with so the boundaries of our friendship stay in place.

Being Known/ Knowing Someone

My parents' marriage is not only a sign of how completely one person can know another person after almost fifty years of marriage, but it is also a symbol of true friendship. When it comes to your own friends, how many people really know you completely? Is there someone who feels fully known by you as a friend? Do you have a buddy (or a girlfriend) who is going to get booted* out of that primary relationship role if your significant other comes along? *(Booted does not mean demotion; it means they are still in your primary circle of friendship; you just have a new primary relationship.) It's easier to make room for a mate if you are already relationally healthy. Here is your relational assignment: Pick three friends who are the closest to your heart, and answer the following questions:

1. Do you know all three people's life stories, including the good, bad, ugly, and glorious?

2. Have you told your version of your story with them in a way that makes you feel they really know you and understand your past?

3. Do you celebrate significant events and moments with them? Birthdays, holidays, awards, accomplishments, etc.? Are you one of the main people they look to and receive affirmation from when they need celebration? (I.e. You plan their promotion party, you give them the gift they have been talking about wanting all year for Christmas, or you post their softball championship status on Facebook because you are so proud of them.)

4. Are you there for them when they are suffering? In sickness, in heartache, in grief, in loss. (I.e. You bring them soup when they are sick or

offer to help them, you are there when they have a breakup, you go to their grandmother's funeral with them, you buy them Kleenex when their girlfriend dumps them.)

5. When they need their identities affirmed, are you one of the people who adds to their sense of strength?

6. Do they do 2, 3, and 4 for you as well?

7. Since relationships only work if both sides communicate needs, have you had talks from time to time about what is working and what is not?

8. Do they get your inside jokes, and you theirs?

If you don't have anyone who meets these relational requirements now, it means someone is going to have to help you create your relational abilities instead of just developing a relational future with you. That is a lot of pressure to give someone. Look around your world and see who you can deliberately start to be a friend to.

I Kissed Dating Goodbye, Then Asked It Out Again . . .

Before you throw this book in the trash or write me Christian hate mail, or post a monster criticism based on the chapter's title, let's look at three very different definitions of dating—the secular view, the religious perspective, and God's viewpoint.

I think **the world's definition of dating** is:

- ☐ Finding someone to be happy with and enjoy—hopefully for a lifetime, but maybe just for today (or tonight).
- ☐ Shopping for that potential someone to spend your life with, or hook up with, or try out.
- ☐ Having an encounter with someone based on sexual chemistry.
- ☐ Saying to a girl, "How you doin'?" and hoping she responds to your desires (to no longer be alone/to have a better life based on the American dream/to have immediate gratification from the opposite sex without any long-term hope).

Almost everyone has a fantasy of what marriage should be like, and the relationship process that gets us there is horribly lopsided. People cycle through the opposite sex faster than they cycle through the bicycle portion of the Ironman Triathlon. The main reason why is because there is very little taught in society about commitment. With 40-50 percent of marriages ending in divorce in America, it is obvious this generation does not understand dating or marriage. I have met some non-Christian couples who have better marriage skills than Christians because they give love a higher place of honor than their needs and desires. Love is a gift from God for everyone, and all marriages require a skill set that includes honor and commitment.

I think **the religious spirit's definition of dating** is:

No! Wait! Scratch that dating word!

Courting

(better to use a Christian word to separate ourselves from danger)

☐ The desire to be fulfilled by one's mate, fulfillment meaning to live the most amazing life of having babies and populating your church meetings.

☐ Meeting someone who all the key people in your society and religious world approve of.

☐ Getting married as soon as possible (because it is the only goal).

☐ Meeting someone in hopes they are your absolutely perfect counterpart (which will allow you to accomplish all of God's greater goals for your life, and without them you might cease to exist at some point).

☐ Meeting someone God tells you is *The One*, then rushing through intimacy building and calling it courtship.

☐ Dating without the fun of dating. (Oh, snap)!

When I was a young Christian man, our church embraced some very conservative theology about relationships, and because of this, the ladies in our church embraced it too. Needless to say, my chances with those girls were zero to none unless I was willing, on the first date, to say I was courting them to marry them. I refused to do that. Luckily, our church was not so religious and conservative it made the girls wear old women's garb and cover their heads and show no signs of makeup —that was my good friend's church. I think he's gay now.

I appreciate that we were religious in our church, but we lived in California, so there was some balance when it came to what the girls had to conform to. The homeschooled friends I had during my high school years never had the chance to date anyone because they were taught an almost sixteenth century viewpoint of culture, which included a very religious form of dating. This meant their date had to drop out of the sky and say, "Marry me!" right off the bat. Who could they ever get to know as a friend? Those poor homeschooled kids didn't even have a chance. Most of them are still unmarried. Obviously, many homeschooled kids today do not have this problem because there are many different parenting types of homeschoolers. My homeschooled friends, on the other hand, were not necessarily kids who represented the norm; they were more of the extreme kind. *(Whisper: at least, I hope so.)*

I think **God's definition of dating** is:

☐ Pursuing (or being pursued by) someone who is qualified to be interested in you.
☐ Getting to know someone you are attracted to (both spiritually and naturally) with the desire/hope for a love to develop that *might* (key word = might) lead to marriage.
☐ Bonding with someone in order to get to know him/her and to learn if you could possibly share life together.

Here is where I will offend many, but hopefully it will all work out. God invented dating. He created a process of pursuing, alluring, and provoking love in the one you are spiritually and sexually attracted to. This has worked out differently in every culture, and each culture has its strengths and limits about the subject, but God inspired the idea of romance. He loves romance, and the D word was His long before it was the world's or Satan's.

God is a relational God. He loves love; it's what He speaks about most. God, Himself, spoke romantically all through the Bible to continually woo Israel, His covenant people. It was a process of dating/courtship that required defined steps. Each season of God's pursuit was very different, so there was form applied to each one with no standard model. God, Himself, dated Israel! This is important to understand. He knew already He was going to inherit the bride for Himself, but He still used romantic language to woo her. He understands love's quest.

A Christian cuss word: dating

Every relationship has a process, so let's talk about the religious process of dating. Where do these churches get their dating rules from? Many church people who write materials or standards on dating have never used them in their own relationships. A lot of what they write is in reaction to weakness as opposed to being written for the sake of truth and enjoyment of life. The vast majority of the church has overreacted to the worldliness of secular dating, and has put up such stringent rules for getting into a relationship that singles often get stuck being single. Many of these rules require you to have some sort of knowing from heaven that says, "This is *The One* for you *forever!*" (insert trumpet sound here) before you even start getting to know the person.

Of course, that scenario only happens when the ones who have supposedly heard from God actually tell their objects of desire they are interested which, in some Christian circles, can take months . . . no, years of the burning desires brewing to the point of insanity. (We will talk about this scenario later . . . it can create a Christian form of stalking.) Once you tell the object of your desire he/she is *The One*, a clunky courtship ensues, and it continues on to its destiny (of marriage), whether you discover he/she is a psycho or not.

Before you hate on me . . . if we were only motivated to be in a relationship with Jesus because we wanted to go to heaven, it would be a truly terrible and boring relationship. It would be based on need/fear/freedom from hell instead of love/intimacy/union with God. Most of us treat dating this way, because our ultimate motive is just to get married to someone.

In a male/female relationship, whenever the focus is on something other than just building relationship it becomes unbalanced, because the relationship is not built on a foundation of intimacy and friendship. Let me be real. If you are going to spend the rest of your life with someone of the opposite sex, then God wants to give you the time and enjoyment of getting to know him/her without the brain strain of planning your whole wedding on the first date.

So how do you form a godly standard of getting to know someone you are interested in? How many times are you allowed to date without looking like a church hussy? (We coined this term "church hussy" because most church members start to look bad to the rest of their congregation after they have dated more than three people in the church. They look especially bad if one date was one of the pastor's adult children.) Many churches are far too awkward in their relationship habits. It's not wrong for you to get to know people!

Who's in charge?

When you read this next statement, it is not written so you will cast off restraints and close your ears to your authority figures. **If you are an adult, then you are in charge of the relationships you build**.

I am not inviting you to rebel against your leadership or your parents or family unit. It is funny that I would even need to qualify this, or that it would concern people. We (adults) shouldn't be afraid to give you your freedom—it's what you deserve as an adult. This is one of the reasons why I have written this book: a religious mind-set is getting in the way of the joy of freedom.

There are too many national and religious cultures promoting relational choices that are not based on reality and are unhealthy. So many people submit themselves in wrong ways by trusting their parents or spiritual overseers too much—they let others dictate their (possible) future lives and destinies with the people they are pursuing or being pursued by. I know people who let their parents or pastors have so much authority in this process that they don't even think for themselves about it; they just coast on autopilot to other people's decisions. That hasn't worked out for anyone I know too well. As an adult you are responsible for the way you build your relationships. At the end of the day, God will hold you responsible for the relational choices you made. You have to make up your own mind. Romantic relationships are not supposed to be directed by your parents or by the ministry you are involved with (although they may be inspired by them).

You have the freedom to set your own standards

You and I both know relationships are the most precious things that we have, besides the first commandment. That means God, Himself, wants to interact with you about them. We need to desire interdependent, loving, sacrificial relationships. You are in charge of how to have them, when to walk away from them, when to commit to them, etc.

Let me state this:

> ## Unless you have a bad moral foundation or some major character issues, then you have the freedom to set your own standards in the relationship process.

God will mentor you. Yes, it will help you to hear healthy stories from those around you who are experiencing good marriages or relationships. Yes, sometimes their models and theological structures can inspire you. Yes, you will need advice, help, counsel, and friendships from role models; but you can't be bound to someone else's interpretation of your own personal process. If you get addicted to someone else's opinions or desires for you, then your happiness is dictated by their approval, not your own.

Are you going to let others steal your relationship process by imposing their standards on you? Are you controlled, either internally or by others, by a religious dating mindset which binds you to others' opinions? Their opinions are wrapped around your own choices, thus violating yours. You need to have the freedom to choose to pursue God, and others, in a way that is different to others' standards, even if you share the same core values.

If you read books or go to seminars on relationships, then make sure to get a balanced perspective beyond just one model. It is easy to substitute relational processes with formulas that may actually not develop a passionate relationship. Yes, there are people you respect whose advice is based on their own stories, but their stories are only examples of what your relationships could be like. **Since every relationship is radically different, the process of each relationship will be too**. So, if you are feeling bound by someone else's desire or model for you, I hand you freedom—the freedom to set your own relationship model first, and let theirs be an additional inspiration to what is true in your own heart!

We need to have a balanced perspective when setting goals to pursue significant others. Repeat after me: **I am in charge of the relationship processes of my life.**

A leader's responsibility

As a leader, it is not my job to set standards in other adults' lives, but I am supposed to help guide them into creating their own standards. People will only live or die by the standards they have set for themselves through interpretation of the Scripture, and through imitating the good they see in balanced relationships (ones that have accountability and love). When I set standards for people, they never fully own them in a life and death way. Instead, the standards just become good principles in their heads. Put it this way: If I help someone get married primarily out of my desire for them, then it means when they go through a hard time, I have to help maintain their relationship by counseling them and convincing them to stay together

What's the goal?

Do you know it's ok to get to know someone you are interested in without having to visualize him/her at the altar? Of course, it's good to be interested in the person for the desire of marriage, but this desire cannot be desperate. It cannot be a consuming focus. The relationship itself has to be the goal, not the progression of where the relationship will lead you.

We need to talk about a balanced way to pursue a person you are physically/spiritually attracted to. I have spent many hours hearing awesome dating life stories from Christians who are now married. I have also walked next to some who are now hurting from painful and unbalanced relationships. So what are the safety nets that will keep you . . . um . . . safe when it comes to going forward or backing out, even if it's not mutual? We are going to look at this question in future chapters. Keep reading!

Making Your List, Checking It Twice

Like I said in the previous chapter, the relationship, itself, has to be the first goal, not the progression of where the relationship will lead you. So how do you set standards which help you to get into realistic and healthy relationships? How do you maintain these standards yet keep them flexible? How do you pursue someone who you are qualified to date and who is qualified to date you? How do you set a standard of getting to know someone in whom you are interested, in a clean way? How many times are you allowed to go through this without looking like a church hussy?

Setting standards before you start a relationship

I think that before you get into a relationship, it's good to get an idea of what you know you want. Although you can't draw a detailed picture of what you want in a relationship, you can build a skeletal view of what you want it to look like. What are your values for a lifelong relationship? How do you define standards without being idealistic?

Developing your standards: making a relational plan

It's time to create a checklist of what you want in a lifelong friend (and possible future spouse). You can divide it into a few categories. Below, I will show you a few of my friends' checklists (which may be totally different to yours. That's the beauty of it all—the individuals in every marriage are different, and each one has unique desires).

Greyson's checklist:

- [ ] A woman who will love to partner with him in life. He doesn't want a separate life from her, or a trophy wife who only serves him and makes him look good. He wants a companion, both in life and in business.
- [ ] A woman who wants to start up and complete huge projects with him.

- A woman who wants to raise a family, and who wants to raise the kids together purposefully.
- Someone who has a really fun personality and who is not passive.
- Someone who loves the arts because she loves creative expression. She could be a dancer, singer, painter, or she just appreciates art, but she should be someone who has pursued this.
- Someone who either values or can value the athletic lifestyle he loves.
- Spiritually, someone who is very self-motivated and has a Christian foundation.
- Someone who can challenge him intellectually.
- A woman who will be his best friend.

Matilda's checklist:

- A man who is very masculine. She loves a man's man and doesn't want a skinny man who wears women's jeans and is in a *band*.
- A man who loves to dance and go out. She doesn't want a homebody.
- A man who loves his career but includes her in the decision-making processes of his life.
- A man who loves adventure and wants to travel, because she loves to see the world.
- A man who will want to reach out to the poor all over the world with her because she needs someone to partner in justice with her.
- A man who loves family and will love her family as much as she does.
- Someone who values administrating life and planning time together with wisdom.
- Someone who is spontaneous, but not all the time.
- Spiritually, a man who loves to support and serve her church to see its goals and purposes actually happen.
- A man who loves to give financially, just as she does, and has a high value in helping children.
- A man who will help her stir up her dreams.

Mark's checklist:

- ☐ A smart woman who will track with him but who may also have a completely opposite personality to his. Mark is an intellectual who loves the pursuit of education.
- ☐ Someone with strong family values who understands what a healthy family looks like (to give their future family a base of strength. Mark didn't have a strong family).
- ☐ A woman who won't try and change him even if she doesn't want to engage in his love of fantasy and sci-fi.
- ☐ A woman who can make a home feel like a home.
- ☐ Someone who loves animals and believes in animal rights, just as he does or at least supports him in this.
- ☐ Spiritually, someone who inspires people.
- ☐ Someone who, like him, wants to be involved in ministry.

Loretta's checklist:

Loretta has two kids from a previous marriage so she has some pretty special needs. At the same time, she doesn't want to settle for less just to have someone carry the family with her.

- ☐ A man who is independent and is skilled in making good financial decisions and life choices.
- ☐ Someone who is very responsible and can open his heart—this is so important to her.
- ☐ A man who she can be honest with and who she feels safe with.
- ☐ A man who is able to play and enjoy a childlike heart.
- ☐ A man who isn't intimidated by her success (she has a very high-paying job). She doesn't mind if he makes less as long as it doesn't affect their relationship.
- ☐ A man who loves people and is sociable.
- ☐ Someone who has a good social network to bring to the marriage because she is bringing incredible relationships that God has given her.
- ☐ Spiritually, she values community and emotional progression in

life, so she wants a man who knows how to motivate himself to dig deep in God and grow in character.

Obviously, these people may not get all of their desires met by one person, but it's a great skeleton for them to pray into and ask for. Is it unrealistic to find someone who matches a lot of these, or at least half of these? No, not in our culture. We, in the Western world, have a great opportunity to have high standards that are defined by our hearts. We may have someone come along whose character, personality, likes, and dislikes match nothing on our skeleton list, but they should at least have the same basic values we do.

So now it's time for you to develop your checklist.

Checklist of things to think about
- ☐ The spiritual strengths you want the person to have
- ☐ Personality strengths and character strengths which are important to you
- ☐ Life pursuits or goals you would like to share with your potential mate
- ☐ Things you always dreamed he/she would be like
- ☐ Things you don't want to live without

Finding yourself on someone else's checklist
Perhaps you've been reading these lists in total dismay because you are (or you think you are) a combination of everything these four people don't want in a lifelong friend/spouse. All is not lost. It will take some time, but we are all made from the same source, and we are all capable of relational greatness.

"God Told Me I'm Going to Marry You." or "I'm Gonna Get YOU Sucka!"

So you've made your list and you already think you know who *The One* is, and you've completely ignored everything I've already written about not making marriage your goal. You don't think it's in any way important to consider all the things I'm talking about because if God the omniscient is telling you who *The One* is, then you need to just go get engaged already and forget about the clumsiness of dating, right?

This chapter deals with the subject of God telling Dick to marry Jane when Dick and Jane are not even in a relationship. It is about faith journeys into marriage, or believing you know who you are going to marry without ever having considered the whole picture of the other person's will and desires.

Her hormones spoke and said, "I am God, listen to Me! He is your husband, and oh, by the way, you need to eat some chocolate right now."

The source

When we train people in hearing God's voice, we have to teach a lot about the source of what we hear. I am not worried about training the average Christian (who has a decent foundation) how to shut down a false voice. It is hard for the Christian to really pay attention to a negative spiritual voice because it is usually so obvious. What is hard is when Christians hear the voice of their own desire or are influenced by their own attractions and hormones, and they hear based on what they *feel*.

Because hormones and desires are so much a part of you, they are usually the most misleading influences in your quest to hear God about relationships. They are ingrained in your nature, and so, when you ask God a question about something you are very passionate about and it involves desires in your heart or hormones or physical desires, WATCH OUT! Sometimes your hormones sound just like God! They can have the same quality of tone to the voice in your head! This is frustrating for many people who are trying to hear God's still small voice in their hearts. Sometimes the voice we hear can lead us into the very will of God, but at other times we haven't developed our listening skills enough to know when the voice's words are the opposite of reality or wisdom.

Your heart is not evil

There is an old theology that says you are impure and your heart's desires are wicked. This may be true if you don't know Jesus, but when you are walking with God, your heart grows in goodness. This means you can begin to trust the nature of Christ inside you as you grow into it. It's not going to happen overnight. There has to be a steady progression of growth so that you can begin to trust the new heart you are in the process of receiving.

If you come into your Christian walk weak in an area, you need to take time to get strong in that part of your mind and heart before you can trust the voice you hear. If you have experienced negativity and brokenness in your relationships with others, you will probably start out hearing more of your own desires, or even self-preservation, speaking to you. You won't hear very clearly from God when you talk to Him about dating or marriage *until* your heart and mind heal from the pain and dysfunction of your broken relationships. It works the same way in other areas in life, such as finances, transitional decision making, etc.

Sometimes we hear from the big guy instead of the big God; they aren't the same, men!

So many people who feel they have had a vision or heard from God about who they are supposed to marry have never heard God on a big level about anything else. But now, out of the blue, they feel they have heard God and believe it 100 percent wholeheartedly because . . . well . . . because they want to.

So guys (or girls), you have heard from God about who you are going to marry. *Don't listen to Beyoncé! Don't go buying that engagement ring just yet!* How do you really know you have heard? What is the checks-and-balances system you have put in place to weigh and judge what you heard? Do you realize that when you are growing in hearing God's voice and He tells you anything that has real information in it, you need to develop a track record of accuracy before you act on the bigger things like hearing from God about marriage?

If you are going through a sexually-frustrated period, it is easy to manufacture a voice in your hormonal head, so be careful. The voice's origin is probably coming from a lower place in your body than your heart.

What happens when you don't have a track record?

One church in a Latin-American country had a woman who began to prophesy. She was a family member of the pastor, so that gave her more credibility. She said God told her a tsunami was coming to their city and it was going to destroy everything on a specific date. They warned the mayor, it was on the news, and everyone began to invest in properties outside that city. You know what? The day came and went and the tsunami forgot to come!

Her friends and family tried to console her by telling her they had repented as a nation just right. (No one remembered ever doing a national day of repentance; no one even remembered hearing of one church repenting. There was no revival in the city as evidence of the repentance. Maybe they just didn't want her to be disappointed.)

Some of her church friends told her they had so much power in prayer they stopped it. (The church had fewer than one hundred people who were not having regular prayer meetings . . .)

Probably, though, her friends and family didn't tell her the most likely answer: She didn't really hear from God. See how complicated these things get?

The church lost its good reputation and people don't trust the integrity of her ability to hear from God anymore. I asked the pastor if the woman had ever heard God about anything before, told people, and then it came true? It was the funniest pastoral answer I have ever heard. In an almost Spanglish accent he said, "Not specifically."

This is similar to you hearing God speak to you about marriage without a personal track record. It's what happens to you when you say God told you, but then God doesn't tell the other person and you find out you are wrong. You lose credibility with friends and family and, more importantly, the opposite sex. Most importantly, you can lose trust in God, when it really was foolish to believe the voice you heard in the first place.

Have you ever predicted a tsunami and it happened? How about a drizzle? You'd better get a track record before you believe you know who you are going to be married to, because in your world, for the rest of your life, it's that big of an issue—it's a tsunami.

David killed a bear and a lion before he tackled a man. Girls, you should too!

(This is my favorite line in the book! I hope I get quoted on the internet forever for writing it.)

And guys, take the example as well. If God is going to speak to you about marriage, He is also going to prepare you by giving you *tangible* confirmations and witnesses in unprecedented ways.

Again what is your checks and balances system? Here are some good ones:

1. Have I heard from God about major things before? How about minor things? How about anything on which I can track real, tangible fruit?

2. Am I a person prone to fantasy?

3. How do some mature believers feel about this?

If I told a mature Christian, in another church that is like mine, the whole story—that I have heard from God and I am promised to another person—would they think it sounded ridiculous based on my amount of confirmation? Would it sound rational? (Our own family and friends love us so much that sometimes they will go along with anything, even the best and most mature of them.)

4. Have I been lonely lately? Was I born lonely?

5. Do I believe my mate is going to make my whole life begin? Will he/she complete me? (See Chapter 1—Being Successfully Single.)

6. Do I have a remote chance with this person? Do they know I even exist?

I have known many women who see a single Christian minister and, as he bares his heart, they hear the voice of their yearning hearts say, "You are called to marry this one, my daughter." The sad thing is, there is no way they will ever meet this person. They begin to fantasize about what their marriage will be like. This is unhealthy. *You probably shouldn't be fantasizing about marriage with someone unless you are in a relationship with him/her. Don't set yourself up for disappointment.*

7. Have you suffered from a lot of rejection by the opposite sex?

One of my guy friends had been rejected by girlfriends so many times that he wanted to leave it up to God to pick him the perfect mate. He went into his room and prayed and saw what he thought was a vision of a girl in his home group. He believed she was *The One,* based on this experience. It took him two years and her getting married to someone else to realize he hadn't heard from God. When I asked him about it, after he got some counseling, he said, "It was just easier to believe a fantasy that felt so big and unreal than to walk through any more rejection."

8. When I heard this, what was the fruit of it? Did it make it easier to pursue the person or did it complicate it?

Most of the time, when it is fantasy or hormones we hear, it complicates the process of getting deeply involved with someone. It isolates us from them.

9. Is this person out of your league?

Not in the world's social standpoint, but in reality. Is it a person who would typically never marry you because you're obviously not their type? We have to look at the natural realities, even if God sometimes chooses to supersede them in someone's heart.

I know a single minister in his forties who is a great-looking catch of a guy. He has had many women believe they are called to marry him—women who come from a life of complete brokenness; women with little to no healing; women who wear their brokenness in their body, on their faces, in their social skills, etc. Some of these women have stalked him. It is such a distraction for someone in a prominent position to have adoring fans become adoring stalkers—women who would never truly have a chance with the person, but they have a fantasy of what it would be like to be married to him/her. The odds are, if you have a promise to marry someone who has a reputation, it is probably the magnetism of what the person represents that attracts or draws you to him/her.

Promises of marriage. Do they exist?

It is very rare people would hear from God about their marriages before they even know the person they think they are supposed to marry. That is why there is a process of courting, dating, seeing someone, or whatever you call it in your circle. Let's think about this, though. Not everyone is *called* to be married; most of us have a choice. If you are called into a marriage, it is because the marriage, itself, has a particular purpose. Maybe your marriage is going to be on display as a healthy marriage; maybe you will have children only you two can raise together; maybe you have to partner together in a ministry or you share a secular calling; maybe it's a little of all of these. Sometimes the calling on a marriage is so specific that God goes out of His way to create a testimony out of it.

All of the ways God calls us to anything are awesome, but sometimes He makes a special point in a call so as to showcase. God might call some into a relationship with Him in an extravagant way. (All stories of salvation are awesome, but some stories shine in our generation.) Some are called to ministry by a voice speaking from a burning bush, or they are told how to exercise their ministry calling by getting visual blueprints downloaded into their minds. When God called Jeremiah, the way He did it was very specific and sovereign-like because He had a specific and sovereign purpose for Jeremiah.

In the case of marriage, God *might* speak to Dick very specifically about Jane, when Dick doesn't even know her as a friend, and call him to a promise of marriage; however, if He did, Dick might feel very powerless until it happened. That's not an exciting thing. It would mean Dick would have to believe, with a gift of faith, that God was calling him, even if Jane didn't know him or wasn't feeling it. It would mean Dick would need major confirmation and sustainment for such a hard journey. It would mean suffering and hardship.

I think all Christians want this type of story because they are so idealistic. Idealism is in play when you believe you will finally get the (ideal, perfect, unrealistic) things you have hoped for. Faith is in play when you believe you will finally hold in your hands the (realistic) things you have hoped for.

Sometimes you can think that because you have such hope it means you have great faith. For many people, their hope is not grounded in faith.

Wouldn't it be awesome if everyone had the gifting of Billy Graham? Yet how many people do? Wouldn't it be incredible if everyone's marriage was as prophetically perfect as Rebekah's? While we are supposed to be provoked by these public and biblical examples of God's glory, that doesn't mean we will have the same renown in our own lives. We are supposed to believe, in faith, for God's highest blessings and favor, but we cannot assume our idealistic and unrealistic expectations are better than those God is offering us.

Anyone who is good at playing an instrument would love to be a rock star, but only a few can become a real rock star. A gas-station attendant can hope to win the lottery, but as far as Google can tell, only one attendant has ever won in all the years of US lottery wins. Hoping you are going to marry a literal princess, by faith, is like this. Once you can be realistic about the odds of God using your call to marriage to showcase His glory, you can be freed from idealistic ways of thinking.

Battle of the Sexes

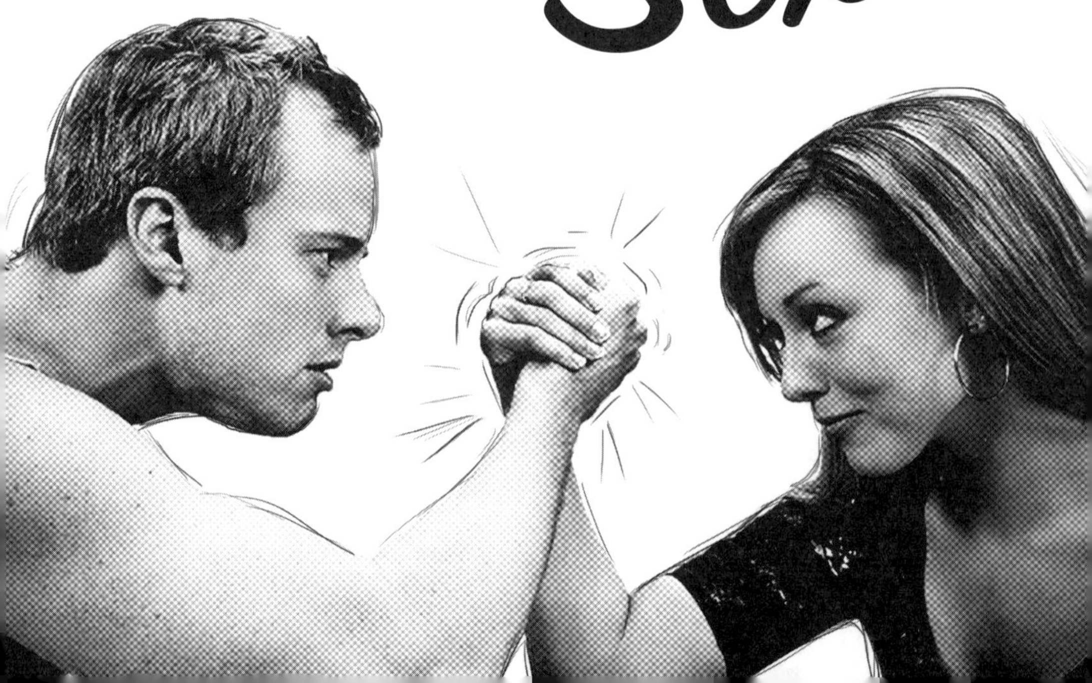

Shawn, the Woman Whisperer, Talks to the Men

I want to talk about how to treat the opposite sex. This chapter's for the guys (waves hands back and forth and snaps his fingers like his friend La Quisha).

I'm going to try and represent the girls' side. I am a guy, so I may fail, but I want to give guys some clues that might take their brains out of neutral when it comes to feminine common sense. I grew up with sisters who were always giving me insight on their womanly ways, whether I wanted it or not.

Women, as you read the following chapters you can either scream out loud in celebration that at least one guy understands, or hate me through Facebook later; either way, my intentions were good. I wish there was a "like" button for my following comments like there is on Facebook. I made my own. Circle it, girls, if you like it.

Treating women with respect is not forcing them into a weaker sex role

Women love to be treated with respect and honor. Each woman is different—some like doors opened for them, others want to open doors for you. What is important from the get-go is to find out, even in friendship, how each particular woman wants to be treated. Does she want you to follow old-fashioned dating rules and walk on the outside of the sidewalk to shield her from oncoming traffic? Or does she not even care about anything but having you look her in the eyes when you talk? A girl will feel honored if you ask her, at the beginning of a relationship, what some of her relational values are.

I dated one girl who wanted old-fashioned chivalry, and another who felt I was wasting time doing it. Each woman is different, and the things that make each one feel like a lady are never going to be exactly the same. The bottom line is: try to please the one you are with, and affirm her by continuing to learn what makes her feel valued.

Most women don't want to be treated as the weaker sex. They want to be viewed as partners to men and partners in life (unless they are Amish and live in towns that don't believe in modern conveniences like electricity and toilets). You have to view them as being equal in value, regardless of your theology on who the head of the relationship is. In other words, even if they believe the theology that states a man is the head of a house, they do not take this as a statement that the man is more valuable or has more rights there. Like?

Girls may experience emotions in a different way than men do, but it doesn't mean they are emotionally unstable

One of my buddies is shut down emotionally, so he doesn't get when his girlfriend cries at chain e-mails about puppies. She is always touched by love, and that touch seems to massage her tear ducts. Instead of this being endearing to him, it has made him uncomfortable, so he pokes fun at her. Is he making fun of her because she is doing something that is weak, or is it because he is insecure about his own emotional process, or lack thereof?

Women tend to be feelers, and they can emotionally process things quicker than most men. God gave them the gift of nurture—their minds and hearts are geared towards heart processes and comfort more than problem solving and strategy. Men need to value and treasure women's emotions. Women want to be able to express themselves without having men "fix" them with their strategic wit. I can't tell you how many times I've watched the phenomenon of how my female friends talk themselves through their own problems. All they want me to do is listen and love on them as they do it—they just need love to be a safe processing place for them. I know, I know, the mystery of a woman's mind, right? Like?

Women have a sex drive

I know, *shocking*. Women lust, and some have porn problems. Many of them masturbate, just like men (well, not in the same way, but . . . don't expect a Christian sex book from me until after I am married for ten years, and only then if I prove to be the champion in bed that my virgin mind wishes me to be). Women want to be touched and felt, sometimes as much as men. This is a very sexual generation, but then again, sexuality has always been around; we are all sexual creatures.

Many men do not understand that they have a responsibility to not only keep their own pants zipped, but to keep their hands in safe places on a woman. A gal is not going to remove your hands because of her own lack of sex drive. She may remove them if she can stand in her convictions of purity, but to put the pressure on her to be the sexually strong one is going to leave you both crossing lines, and that's not fair on either of you.

Women may not be as visual as men, but any one episode of Sex in the City will show you the raunchiness that a girl's mind can host. Christian women may choose purity, but that doesn't mean they didn't go through the sexual awakening of puberty (probably earlier than you). Women think about sex too, their minds just process it differently than men's. Just like single guys would like to have sex while still single, so would single women, especially as they get older. They can experience their own version of sexual frustration.

Women, though, don't just want to procreate; they want to be physically adored and loved. As men, we have a responsibility to not take advantage of this desire and need. Like?

Woman whisperers don't exist

I believe in the horse whisperer. I believe in the dog whisperer. I *do not* believe in the woman whisperer. The title is *totally sarcastic*. Don't assume you know more about women than the next guy. What you experienced with one woman may or may not carry over to the next. Just because you are good at getting an introduction or making up lines that open conversations, it does not mean you will be an amazing partner once you are in a relationship. Each one will take a unique process that no other relationship can recreate. You can use your experience, and even refer to past relationships, but nothing can substitute the process that each woman needs to feel more than acquainted to you. I think women intuitively know that each relationship is different, whereas men try to follow patterns of learned experience.

The Five Love Languages is a book I highly recommend. One love language that all women have is the need for quality time from their significant others. A lot of men need this too, but their need is not as universal as women's.

If you are getting into a relationship, you must be prepared to treat it as a *time commitment*. That means you are going to have to give quality time in *large* amounts, now and for *the rest of your life*. It means that soon, you are going to have to give more time to this woman than you give to anything else (outside of work and sleep). Are you ready for that? Like?

Women need you to be clear when you make a move

Facebook posting to say hi is not a clear signal you are interested in her. Texting her with *"Hey, I just watched another episode of American Idol. That one girl can sing!"* at 10:00 p.m. might look like you're promoting your interest in her, but it is still just a text. Sitting next to her in a group setting can be flirtatious, but the reality is that she is most likely not going to take this as a clear move.

If you like a girl, you need to come out and tell her, e.g. "I am interested in you." "I would love to hang out with you and get to know you better because I like you." "You are amazing. Can we spend time together, because I have feelings for you?" *Send clear signals.*

Clear signals don't mean strong or overbearing signals. A woman does not need you to state your unending love before you win her heart. You don't have to tell her she is *The One*; as a matter of fact, that would be creepy.

She wants to be pursued and treasured, but how can she feel treasured if you haven't even opened her heart up with your goodness yet? Start small but real. Real is the key. Just be direct, and allow her to respond to your directness.

Flirting (innocent expressions of flirting are part of every budding romantic relationship) is fine in the beginning, but you need to make a clear move when you are ready to pursue her; otherwise, you are playing games with her heart. Like?

Lastly, women don't want to have to be the spiritual leader of the relationship

There are so many unbalanced relationships in which the woman has to be the strong one in the pursuit of spiritual things. Women want a spiritual equal. They don't want to have to get you to go to meetings or be your ticket to church. They don't want to always be the one to initiate prayer with you. They want a counterpart. They want a man who knows how to be a man of God. Like?

You may not know what a woman wants, but that is part of the fun about getting to know one. It's the ultimate conquest, the greatest treasure hunt . . . and a woman who is the object of your adventure enjoys the process *if* you treat her with value and keep the lines of communication open.

What Women Want;
The Exam

1. Women watch *The Bachelor* to understand the nature of a man.

   True or false?

2. Women want you to watch romantic chick flicks with them.

   True or false?

3. Women want you to give up your hobbies so they can fully possess all your time.

   True or false?

4. Women want to schedule your social time.

   True or false?

5. All women are complicated during *that* time of the month.

   True or false?

6. Women are complicated.

   True or false?

Answers

1. False: They watch it to talk about the women who are pursing the man (and you should hear some of those conversations). *The Bachelor* is never about the hot guy; it's about the drooling women who have lost their minds, in a competition that is part beauty pageant, part social experiment.

2. True: Women love cuddling up next to you in a theater to watch their favorite actor/actress couple go through a persevering struggle of romance—it makes them feel like both of you can make it into ultimate happiness. They feel bonded to you when you watch love play out together.

3. False: Women really just want your focus and balanced time management. If they don't feel like you are meeting some of their needs, they may not know how to communicate it, so they start to target your hobbies. They see them as competition for the time/affection they aren't sure how to gain from you. If this happens to you, evaluate how you can find out the direct need and begin to meet it (if it's yours to meet).

4. True and false: Many women are looking for relationships that are life giving for you as a couple, so they are more in touch with the types of people that bring out the best in you. They like to arrange time with people that seem to be the most life giving and genuine.

5. False sometimes, but when it's true, it's oh so true: Not all women have these problems, but every relationship has a guaranteed inclusion of a hormonal cycle—one that hits emotions and can cause physical pain. Although some women are very private about this, the odds are that at some point it will be obvious it's that time of the month, whether they like it or not. Part of being a man is being flexible and mature during these times that physically and emotionally exhaust a woman. I have one friend who has agreed with her husband

that she will make no permanent life-altering decisions during this time of her cycle, specifically because she has made some whopping bad mistakes during her hormonally-charged emotional states. The key is to love, no matter how temporarily complicated she gets.

6. True: No explanation needed.

For The Ladies

Girls, ladies, women, queens
welcome to my *For Girls Only* chapter.
I really don't know much about you so
it's going to be very short.

As a matter of fact, that's all I have to say.

God bless!

Ok, ok, I am just kidding, but who knows the mind of a woman that he may instruct her? Only God. At the same time, I want to give you a basic overview about some things guys struggle with and how you can have a balanced relationship. Remember, when I am addressing these things, the reality is we are talking about the *normal* Christian guy, not the extremely broken, perverted, or player guy; because your boundaries would be different with one of those guys, right? Meaning you value yourself more than to date one of them.

Misconceptions and Realities About Guys

Misconception 1: You can't have a real friendship with a guy.

Reality: See my chapter on male/female friendships. When I said we are called to have both male and female friends, it probably shocked some of you.

Misconception 2: You have to be one of the boys to run with the boys.

Reality: As a woman, you understand your need for relationships with men probably more than men do their need with women, because you are more dependant on being able to relate to men in a non-sexual way.

Mainly because of working with men, many women strip themselves of their femininity to relate to men in a non-sexual way, but that's a problem. God made you a female, so I believe you should not have to act any other way. If a man is going to have a problem with your *femaleness*, don't take responsibility for his weakness and lose part of yourself or compromise yourself just because you want peer status. Many female politicians face this problem, and some of them have stripped themselves of femininity so they can run with the boys (not mentioning any names!). Turning into one of the boys so you can have equal authority will, in the long run, cause you great suffering and sorrow. You will know you missed something.

Misconception 3: Guys are always horny and think about sex every seven seconds.

Reality 3: I don't remember what I was going to write because I was too busy thinking about sex . . . not! While this may or may not be true of a guy who doesn't have a good foundation, guys who are pursuing goals and quality relationships do not think about sex with every spare thought.

Sexuality is a normal part of a guy's brain, but that doesn't mean it's a struggle he is wrestling with at all times. It's just part of what he has to process throughout his week—something you may not even think about. For a lot of guys, their sex drive leads them into thoughts which are innocent enough, like a PG-rated preview leads into a full movie and they just enjoy the preview.

Lust is when they pursue these sexual thoughts down a road and they let the thoughts actually engage and entertain them, or they begin to fantasize about them. Lust, in many cases, is not the initial response to what they feel or see; it is the reaction they choose to engage in which causes lust in response. Sexual thoughts are not automatically lust.

This is why some guys might notice a girl's body and it doesn't become lustful in the noticing, it becomes sexual in the re-noticing, and the re-noticing, and the re-noticing, and the picturing, and the fantasizing, etc. As soon as the guy engages the thought is when he lusts. This may be hard for many women to understand, but it is the truth. This leads us into misconception 4.

Misconception 4: If a guy notices your beauty and glances at you, it means he is undressing you with his eyes and picturing you naked.

Reality 4: I have had perfectly innocent friends of mine accused by girls of lusting or undressing a woman with their eyes just because they noticed how pretty she was. If a guy looks at you and is captivated by you, it's just part of him being a man and you being attractive.

If he keeps looking and stays attracted, then you have a problem, unless you like him too. Guys are visual creatures, and just like a woman can look at flowers and it touches a place in her, guys get touched by the beauty of a woman.

The problem is many guys let this go past the God-given desire to see beauty, and it turns into heavy arousal of some sort. It doesn't mean they are physically/sexually aroused, but they might be mentally aroused, and this is, in fact, very uncomfortable for you to feel. It is not evil for a guy to notice your beauty, but it is wrong for him to look and be consumed by it. It is especially wrong for him to stay aroused by it, that is, unless he puts a ring on your finger and walks you down the aisle.

Sometimes girls who have been lusted over in the past feel that every time a guy looks at them they are being used as an object of lust. What is terrible is: I love to look at people. There isn't a sexual drop in my bones when I am in a speaking engagement, but people watching is a passion of mine.

I had one older church-lady-type woman, who was very religious, get mad at me because I was zoned out staring at her, and she felt uncomfortable. She actually said she felt lusted over to the ministry leader. My first reaction in my head was, *Oh my gosh, that's so gross.* But instead of totally offending her and telling her I would rather picture my dogs puke than her naked, I politely informed her she was mistaken and it was her issue, not mine. I think people watching can be fascinating, and to notice someone's physical body is normal. It's the guys who have engaged a perverted view-point who are ruining it for all the others.

Some girls in the church have even stopped wearing makeup or caring about their looks because they just don't want to deal with it. This is so sad to me, because they are letting someone else's problem shut down their enhancement of beauty.

I went through a time when I was working out a lot, and I had quite a few girls noticing me and pursuing me. I literally didn't want to work out any-more because I hated the attention. I dressed frumpily and tried to not even talk to girls my own age. I had bad self-image issues and took this at-tention as negative instead of positive. I had to go through a heart process to take care of myself for the sake of my health, live life at my best, and receive the attention as flattering. Now that I understand that, I need to start working out again!

Misconception 5: Your guy friends who struggle with pornography are secretly lusting over you.

Reality 5: I have counseled many guys, and watched as God got them to a place of freedom from porn and lust. The reality is, there are stages of lust that guys go through, and most of what guys fantasize about is *what is not attainable or close to them*, because there is not the same measure of guilt associated with it.

While popular psychology says most guys even lust after their own moth-ers, my professional opinion is most Christian guys have so much guilt associated with lust they usually won't allow themselves to lust about any-one close to them, so they lust after a fantasy woman instead.

The Lust Scale for Guys

(In these stages I am not addressing homosexuality, fetish, etc., because we are dealing with the commonness of males, not the imbalances or extremes.)

Worst	
Stage 5	Someone close to the guy who is a friend or girlfriend
Stage 4	Someone who is in the guy's life—maybe a school person, co-worker—someone real to them but whom they probably have no chance with
Stage 3	Someone the guy has seen before but doesn't know, someone he has seen throughout the day
Stage 2	Someone in a movie or magazine or on a porn site
Stage 1	A faceless body of a woman/a completely-imagined woman
Stage 0	Thinking about a woman in a way which becomes stimulating
Best	

Most guys will not go past the 0-2 stages of lust, and if they do, it's not often. It's real brokenness which leads us to ongoing daily lust that involves those around us. A man living in balance may touch the 0 stage, but he doesn't make it past that very often.

Not all guys struggle with porn. I, personally, have never had an ongoing struggle with porn over any period of my life, and I am not saying this to boast about my own strength, but so you know not all guys struggle with it. I am surrounded by guys who don't, or guys who are on the winning side of a porn battle, but that doesn't disqualify guys who do. Everyone's struggles are different, and the ones who do struggle with it just need a good skill set imparted to them; and possibly healing of their perspective so they can see porn for what it is: a false sense of intimacy that can block real relational needs from being met.

They can't get this skill set for the most part from a woman. This is primarily a male-to-male issue, or a counselor issue, because it deals with the identity of the man. I know many women who want to help their husbands or boyfriends, but usually this turns out to be very painful for both of them. I think if a man is struggling with porn and is almost married or married, he has an obligation to inform his wife. I think, however, that he should not process it in great detail with his wife, because this can be very hurtful to her. Processing a male-identity sexual weakness needs to be done by someone who can help resolve it.

Don't be naive

I think many girls have gotten into trouble because they have let guys lead the physical relationship, and they don't realize the monster that is defined as a man's sex drive. Many women can kiss and it leads to thoughts of love and romance, whereas much of the time a guy (even a healthy guy) is thinking about getting a physical release. This is why you have to set physical boundaries based on this very real dynamic.

Sometimes a woman who is lonely or desiring affection will allow herself to go to a physical place with a man and have no idea what she has started. It's like unlocking the door, hoping nothing will happen, but knowing he might open that door. Keep the door locked! Don't unlock anything! Take this for what it needs to mean for you!

The important thing is that you realize you and your guy will not be at the same place when you begin any sort of physical relationship. It may equally excite you, but on different levels, and if you open this door, you'd better be prepared to put up strong barbed wire boundaries.

If you are taking a break from the book for the night, my recommended listening is: "Let's Hear it for the Boys" by Cindy Lauper—it will bring depth to this chapter.

7 Things Men Hate!
The Quiz

Let's pretend you are already dating the man of your dreams. We'll watch, and then score you on how much you really now about men . . . Mark the answer you think he'd hate the most.

1. You are going out with a guy and you see a group of women. Your man would hate if you

    A. Noticed how cute they were and commented on their style

    B. Asked him to comment on their shoes or outfit

    C. Made fun of one woman's last-year's-Prada bag, treating her as a rival

2. You had a very hard day, but nothing particular happened to make it world shaking. You:

    A. Can't wait to see your man so you can spend time with him, knowing he can't manage your crisis, but it comforts you that he knows

    B. Call your man over and over, leaving messages about how awful your day has been and then, when you see him, talk about it for at least an hour

    C. Stuff it and have a quality time with your man, hoping he doesn't notice you are upset

3. Your boyfriend goes to the bathroom. His phone flashes with a text message and you see it's from a woman at work. She's on a team with him, but you know she likes him, even if he isn't aware. The text is innocent enough, but you just don't like it. You

   A. Find a way to mention her name at some point during the night to hear his perspective on her

   B. Hold the phone, impatiently waiting for him to come out of the bathroom, then demand he doesn't talk to her

   C. Ignore it, trusting it is just related to church and he isn't a cheater anyway

4. You just spent Monday-Wednesday night with your boyfriend. You know he has Saturday off, but he hasn't mentioned doing anything together yet. You ask him what he is doing and he doesn't seem to have plans. You:

   A. Ask him if he wants to relax with you at your house and spend the day watching movies

   B. Ask him why he doesn't want to spend time with you and why he is avoiding you

   C. Leave him alone and let him have a day to himself, knowing individual time is healthy

5. You are out with your man at the movie theater, which happens to be in a mall with your favorite stores. You know there is a later movie, and you really want to visit the mall. Your man goes shopping with you but he seems uninterested in what you are trying on or what you are showing him. You:

   A. Realize shopping is a woman's sport of choice and decide to come back with girlfriends at your next chance

B. Ask him what he would like to do and wait until something more mutually pleasurable comes to mind

C. Get angry at him for being uninterested; after all, you *are* going to go see *Die Hard 50* with him later

5. You are talking to your man on your second date, telling him about your favorite episode of some teen drama you happened to watch while getting your nails done the other day, and he seems completely bored. You switch the subject to what is happening between your two friends at work, but again, he isn't connecting. You

A. Get mad at him for not being conversationally engaging

B. Get insecure and start thinking maybe you are too boring for him

C. Realize you are having a girl-to-girl conversation and find some-thing that would be more appropriate for a second date

6. While on a date, you notice your guy has not been trained in old-fash-ioned etiquette. He hasn't opened your door, he hasn't walked on the outside of the curb, and he didn't help you sit first, so you

A. Get angry and begin to correct him on everything he is not doing

B. Realize women fought for equal rights and young men rarely get trained in chivalry these days, so you try and get to know him and see if he has honor in other ways

C. Ask him if he would like some simple coaching on some things that would make you feel more like a lady, and then bring your own standards up

Answers
1. c 2. a 3. b 4. b 5. c 6. b 7. a

1–2 Correct: You must have grown up in a monastery on an unknown island in Italy.

3–4 Correct: You went to an all girls' school or had no brothers in your family.

5 Correct: You at least had a date for the prom.

6 Correct: You know your men and have good relationship skills.

7 Correct: You have mad men skills; you understand how to emotionally relate to a man.

Overview of What Men Hate:

1) *When women criticize other females.* When women treat other women as rivals, men get frustrated.

2) *When women try and get men to meet all their emotional needs.* Men don't want to be treated as your emotional doctor. They can support you, but they can't fix everything and everyone. They get irritated when women are constantly needy.

3) *Jealousy.* Jealousy is one of the biggest turnoffs men have. It exasperates them. A jealous woman can break even the strongest relationship.

4) *When women don't allow men to have private time.* Some women want all their men's spare time to be devoted to them alone. A woman is not the owner of a man, she is a counterpart. Men need quiet time.

5) *Shopping for women's things.* They do not want to watch a woman come out of a dressing room with ten to twelve outfits and then look at the twenty-five pairs of shoes which might match each one.

6) *Talkativeness without it being on mutually-engaging subjects.* Women's talkativeness can be really irritating to some men. Women's brains easily conceive every minute detail, while men do not like non-essential details.

7) *Superiority complex.* Women can use their leverage to demonstrate their superiority over men, and it is not pleasant.

Figure It Out

Your turn, men. Let's see if you can mark what dating women love the most.

1. Your girl was singing next to you in the car with all her heart. Her tone was worse than a rejected *American Idol* contestant, but she asks you if you think she can join the worship band at church. You:

   A. Give her a blunt, honest answer: "You might be able to get a recording contract like Milli Vanilli if you don't actually sing . . . "

   B. Lie: "Your voice is like the angels who sing to God, Himself!"

   C. Give her constructive criticism: "I love your enthusiasm for singing; it's fun, but have you ever considered getting your voice trained if you are going to pursue that passion?"

2. You're on your second date with the girl you're interested in. You start the date with:

   A. A funny story you know is enough to make anyone laugh

   B. A run-down of what you did at work and how the day went

   C. The tale of your mother's kidney stones and migraines

3. Your girl looks to you to lead the conversation, and you really don't know what to talk about so you talk about

   A. Working out and getting the right pump on

   B. The thesis paper you worked on in college

   C. Your favorite TV show's plot and what is happening on the show

4. You're on your fifth outing with your new crush, and she is having a terrible day. She shares it with you and you:

   A. Try and tell her jokes

   B. Tell her about your last really hard day

   C. Cheer her up by telling her positive things you've noticed about her and her value

5. You ask your girlfriend where she wants to go for dinner and she says, "Surprise me, baby."

   A. She has never tried sushi, but you are not sure she would like it.

   B. You could go to her favorite place, Tender Greens, which serves salads only (and you're not into salad).

   C. You could try the new steak place down the road you might both like.

6. You are at a sports bar with your buddies. You know you won't have time to finish watching the game, and go to the gym, and get ready before your date tonight. You:

   A. Watch the game to the very end, and then show up in your team's colors, knowing their victory will impress her as well

   B. Go to the gym and get ready, knowing most women will take up to an hour to make themselves look nice for you and you can return the favor

   C. Rush home right after the game and splash on some cologne, wax your hair, and jump into new clothes.

7. You are going to a relationship seminar at church with your lady this weekend, but at the last minute, your best friend wants you to go on an all-expense-paid rafting trip. Your girl has been waiting for three months for this seminar and has been excited, but she would let you go if you really wanted it. You:

A. Pack your car; it's camping trip time

B. Go to the first night of the seminar and leave early the next morning for camping, missing the rest

C. Go to the whole seminar, knowing you can go rafting again sometime soon

8. Your woman believes chivalry is not dead, and she likes the formal way of being treated. You don't know the line so you

A. Ask her to tell you what is important to her and practice those things, like opening car doors for her and opening the house door

B. Tell her women have equal rights and can wear pants too

C. Tell her you never learned it so you don't want to practice it

Answers

1. C. Women like constructive honesty.

2. A. Women love humor, and it's a great way to initiate deep conversation. It's proven when people can laugh together, all the other emotions that happen in a deep conversation are easier to come by.

3. B. A woman is attracted to intelligence—it's one of the most attractive characteristics in any man. What you are interested in can be amazing, even if it's not a common interest, as long as you can read her signals as to when to stop talking about it.

4. C. Women love a positive and sensitive man. By being positive about her value and qualities, you will improve her day, and she won't be able to resist changing her attitude.

5. A. Women like men who will take initiative and take her on an adventure. Even if she ends up not liking the food, she will like the experience.

6. B. Women think physical appearances are important. It's not just men who want an attractive date; women don't want to be seen with a slob. They put effort into their looks for you, and they want to get the same in return.

7. C. Women want to know you will follow through on your word, and they also want to know you care about both your personal and spiritual growth as the relationship develops. By changing plans on something they value, you are communicating where your true priorities lie, and that does not help women to feel safe.

8. A. Old-fashioned chivalry is still greatly appreciated by many women. They like the feeling of being honored and covered, but there are usually contemporary twists which are good to process because sometimes some

of the things can make them feel smothered. Keep communication open about her preferences—this can help the relationship excel.

Disney Romance

So maybe you know what the opposite sex wants. Let's take a further look at what you want.

Disney is my favorite organization. It is my crack, so I have learned much from its movies, especially its romantic themes. There is a lot to learn from Disney movies, even at a young age. Like what, you ask? Like every main character in a Disney movie is an orphan, or has lost one parent, or loses a parent. It's how to get little kids hooked—kill off the parents, make the little guy seem desperate and helpless, and Disney wins the hearts of kids everywhere. Darn baby-manipulating Disney! I digress.

Drip, drip, drop little April showers

I saw *Bambi* when I was a kid, and it inspired many feelings in me. Besides believing hunters were evil until I was around fifteen (don't worry, I have a deer head above my fireplace now named Bambi's Father), I also believed all of nature falls in love in the springtime, and each animal gets its own perfect mate. Wow! Disney made a movie full of sexual chemistry! Even the skunk, who I personally thought was gay, ended up landing a girlfriend!

Oh, that it would be as easy as Disney portrays it to be *(I'm mad at you, Disney, and your deceptive cutesy movies that make love look so perfect)*! The following are lessons learned from the movies I watched growing up.

Cinderella syndrome: "Someday my prince will come."

The bad: One of my friends, an amazing woman, had been praying for her wedding since she was four. She had her hope chest; her photo album full of wedding plans; the names of her children picked out; the rooms in her house preplanned in décor, down to the last detail (it involved hunter green and burgundy walls from the 80's . . . I guess she locked into ugly style from a bad era); her journals packed full of things she would talk to her soon-to-be husband about; and pretty much everything she needed . . . except a man to share it with.

She lived in the fantasy of a marriage of lifelong romance, but had never even gone to a school dance with a guy. As a matter of fact, she made her plans known to all of her closest girl and guy friends, telling them all what Mister Right looked like and how romantic he was going to be with her. She was socially awkward around potential guys because she had made herself fundamentally un-pursuable. She was waiting for the perfect Prince Charming, and she would *know* when he showed up; therefore, she was single into her late thirties.

At one point, she was so disappointed that she came to us for prayer. I felt we needed to have a book burning of all the plans she had made because they were floating around in the Cinderella castle of her mind, far, far outside the truth of real relationships. She had so much control over her fantasy there was no room for reality in it anymore. I told her I felt sorry for any guy who tried to pursue her because her standards were so ridiculously high—he would have to have been Superman to break into her citadel. It was time to divorce imaginary Prince Charming, who her mind had married, so she could find Normal Ned. (I like that name . . . Ned.)

Other Cinderella-type girls and guys are people who feel as if they are victims of life. They believe they will be saved from normalness when some magical mate comes around to rescue them, and then everything wonderful in life will begin. This *Cinderella syndrome* plagues the church. Do you realize that if you are bored in your normalness then you are probably not going to get rescued from it? Who wants someone who doesn't like his/her own life and even bores him/her self? Your first steps in your quest for your Prince Charming need to be:

- □ begin a season of learning who you are
- □ pursue your passions
- □ fall in love with Jesus

The good: What we learn from *Cinderella* (especially as Christians) is that our social class, or lack thereof, does not define our value. We are all royalty, and we are all worthy of happiness. Cinderella was a little girl who became quite the catch because her identity was formed and she believed in herself.

So many people are on this journey. Right now you may feel like a cleaning lady no man will notice, but if you find great value in yourself you will become noticeable to a caliber of man who dreams are made of. Someday your prince *will* come . . . when you work in the meantime on becoming a version of you you can love and be proud of.

Beauty and the beast-itis: "Every beast deserves a beauty."

The beast sits in his castle all day feeling sorry for himself because he is so ugly, but one day his Beauty will come and cry him into life and love.

The bad: One of my Christian guy friends had been living a pretty wild lifestyle of alcohol and light womanizing (R-rated not X-rated). He was skating on the edge of the world, often crossing the line in his crazy desire to experience it all. He'd get guilty enough about his compromise that he would come back into the church every few months, get passionate for a few weeks, and then repeat the whole cycle. One day I made a joke like, "If you don't quit being a fence-walker, you're never going to marry the type of woman you most desire." I was shocked by his response. He said he was going to marry one of the purest Christian girls in the church, one who had no struggles, and she could settle him down. In other words, he was allowed to live this crazy lifestyle as long as he wanted because in his mind, all the problems would go away when he got married to a Christian woman who would take it upon herself to be his moral barometer. He believed some woman was going to drop into his castle and tame the beast inside him with her endearing love. At this point, I put my phone to his ear and he said,

"Who is it?"
To which I replied, "Your wake-up call," and punched him, hard.

There are many guys and girls who have the *Beauty and the Beast syndrome*. These are people who allow themselves to be rebellious, wild, aggressive, angry, and out of control, yet believe they are going to be rescued by a perfect mate who will come alongside them and balance them out. What a terrible and selfish pressure to put on someone! You're supposed to come into a relationship offering the best of what you have developed in your own life, relationships, and faith—not come at your weakest, hoping his/her strength will compensate!

I have had talks with mothers who are hoping the right girl comes along to tame their wild beast of a son! Do you realize how ridiculous and mean that is to some young woman, who would not only have the pressure of a relationship on her, but would also be in a relationship with a boy who hadn't learned how to take responsibility for his own character? MOM, WAKE UP! Pray your son builds his character on his own, not that some woman comes along to fix him!

The good: Inside each of us is a rough man/woman who is softened and tamed by true committed love. I have seen two people with raw edges and *beastiness* who, through their vow of marriage, helped pull each other higher. The types of character building marriage can bring are unparalleled.

If you have a beast in you and you are teachable, love will be the quickest way to shape your desire to be a better person for that special someone.

Peter Pan syndrome: "I don't want to grow up."

Peter Pan was a wonderful story about a little boy who was very old but still wore tights. I could forgive the moviemakers that, but I couldn't forgive them for making Wendy a mother figure he then fell in love with . . . kinky Disney movies! Actually, it's one of my favorite movies, but not because of that.

The bad: On a serious note, there is a real problem in the world with adults who do not want to grow up and take full responsibility for their lives. One man I know would sacrifice time with his girlfriend almost every day, just to play five to ten hours of online video games. I don't know why she stayed with him. He refused to accept that the real world was more exciting than his online world. She had to play with him online to spend even halfway quality time with him. They even got married in the video game because he was too consumed to marry the *real* girl the right way in *real* life. Eventually she dumped him, and their in-game characters got divorced when she left him for a level-80 night elf fighter. Video games are one of my passionate hobbies, but they don't substitute well for the love of a woman.

So many people choose pleasure and self-absorbed fun over the responsibility of relationship. Another thing people who have *Peter Pan syndrome* do is purposely date someone who overcompensates for their lack of responsibility. In one marriage I know of, the wife has three boys she is raising and only two came out of her—the other one helped make them (the boys' dad). Frankly, it's unfair when one of the parties in a relationship refuses to balance out personal time, hobbies, and fun, and not share time with a (potential) mate.

So if you are The Pan, fly on back to the real world, log on out of that level-seventy dwarf cleric for a while, and come visit the land beyond Azeroth; or holster that VSC Phantom, or even cancel your NFL DirecTV ticket!

The good: *Peter Pan* was a great picture of being with someone who still has an inner child alive and well. Being childish is different from being childlike. Being childlike means you still have awe for life, hunger for experience, and eyes which see everything as new and full of adventure; but you are trainable. Being childish means you avoid responsibility, lack commitment, and won't sacrifice for others because of selfishness. Everyone loves childlike people because they are refreshingly excited about life and don't get stuck in a monotonous rut.

Grow up, but stay childlike.

Sleeping Beauty: " . . . and he kissed her and her life finally started. "

There he found her, asleep because of the sleeping spell of a witch. There was that lump of woman just lying there, perfectly preserved externally, but nothing going on inside. He had finally found the woman of his dreams . . . or had he?

The bad: There is another phenomenon I have seen under the sun: women who don't really live life with any ambition, yet they expect to be rescued by the ambition of their man. In other words, they are asleep in life and have not begun to live yet. Apathetic, dull, indifferent, lazy, ordinary, unexciting, unimaginative, uninteresting, uncreative, uninspiring . . . these traits are some of the more unattractive ones to most men, although not everyone notices why these women aren't attractive.

There is nothing worse than a lifeless woman with *Sleeping Beauty syndrome* waiting for you to kiss her into a real life. Her only ambition is to be your trophy wife and support your ambition; or better yet, she promises to do everything she can in the relationship . . . once you provide financially and become her shield and shelter. In America in particular, this just isn't as attractive as it might have been in the 1950s, when *Sleeping Beauty* was made.

At least it's better than the woman who had seven dwarfed relationships and then finally found her prince to marry but brought the dwarves' baggage into it . . . oh, wait! Snow White wasn't going to be in this chapter.

The good: Sometimes *Sleeping Beauty* can represent people who let their romances stay sleeping until they are mature enough, or ready, for a relationship. She represents the thought of not giving your heart away until you have gone through the very real process of learning how to build relationships. This is a rare one in our generation, but it's a beautiful thing when you are the prince who feels the purity of being the one to awaken that kind of sleeping Beauty.

No love can make you live your life. That's your job.

The Jungle Book: "He has a past, but I like the bad boy type."

Oh, wow! We have a story of a little boy raised by wild animals, but he finds a perfect woman who pulls him back to civilization, and all the while he maintains his relationships with the animal kingdom.

The bad: Doesn't that sound like some of the relationships you have watched? A woman rescues the bad boy, the boy with the terrible upbringing or who lives across the tracks, but he never fully gives up his rebellion or the pain in his orphaned heart? Marriage to a jungle boy is all fun and games until the bears and monkeys he befriended show up . . . Hey! You're the one who is marrying into the jungle.

Know your man. Know his background. Know his weaknesses and strengths. Is he willing to work through and heal from past wounds—maybe some caused by his parents, a broken past, an orphan mindset, or his heart's attitude?

The good: Sometimes someone's negative life experiences can be a great source of strength in a relationship. I have a friend who had abusive parents, and he spent his broken childhood dreaming of the type of father and husband he wanted to be. You know what? He's awesome!

We can use our brokenness and the pains of life to make clear choices on whom we will become; and that, my friend, is the deepest form of character.

The Little Mermaid: "I wish I could be part of that world . . . "

We all know a girl like this. She already has everything. She is the one who has an established, normal, self-sufficient life; but her true walk of adventure and fun will finally start if she can only be a part of *his* world . . . *"Look at this stuff . . . isn't it neat? Wouldn't you think my collections complete? Wouldn't you say I'm the girl, the girl who has everything . . . ?"*

The bad: If she doesn't know how to go on adventures and make her life more exciting now, why is she putting the pressure on a guy to do it for her? Women like her usually have an incredible first year of romance because romance has rescued them from a life full of things (lots of hobbies, a good career, etc). that are not satisfying. The problem is: the romance is better before marriage. Once they settle into relationships, there is no spark left, because romance must be fueled by both sides of a relationship.

The girl who has everything we are talking about values everything around her but sees no value in herself. Acquisition and fantasy have always fueled her passion; it has never come from within. She has to learn how to love herself, value herself, and be the one to fuel adventure first! Then she will bring all kinds of healthy and balanced excitement into a relationship, instead of relying on a frenzied magic moment of losing fins and scales to grow feet!

The good: When we get into a relationship, we change each other's access to the world. Whether you marry someone from another city, or you just have someone bringing his/her unique life experiences, you are bound to become more by joining together. Part of an amazing relationship is inheriting another person's accomplishments, relational sphere, talents, etc. This is exciting, and many people get pumped about what happens when two worlds promise to come together through marriage. This should be an incentive for some people because it can be so powerful.

Overcoming idealism

I was going to use the example from *The Lion King* to demonstrate idealism, but using one of the animal stories felt a little strange in a human book.

Are these examples that extreme? When you look at them, even if you can just barely identify with one of them, it shows how unrealistic you are being. Maybe your syndrome was not described, but do you have unrealistic expectations? How did you set your expectations in the first place?

The problem with most Christians is that we are hopeful dreamers, taught to live by faith and, because of it, we sometimes become extremely idealistic. We begin to mentally conjure up a partner who could only come out of a Disney movie (because no one on earth could match our vision). I think we are more prone to fantasy because we believe God is good and He desires to bring us His best, but we forget God's best will always be a real person. We also believe we can sit back and wait for our Disney soul mate to show up. The moment we meet *The One*, our eyes will meet his/hers and heaven's perfection will be ours. The truth is, though, if we want to begin a relationship, we cannot wait around forever without putting any effort into the pursuing process.

A man I knew made me laugh when he told me his checklist of qualities in a wife. Here is what they were:

- ☐ She has to be as beautiful as a supermodel.
- ☐ She has to be rich.
- ☐ She has to be extremely gifted and talented in many of the arts.
- ☐ She has to be of good family background or important bloodline (royalty, he hopes. Hey, men can have the *Cinderella syndrome* too).
- ☐ She has to love Jesus more than he does.

Now, the problem with his standards was that to find a woman with those qualifications, when he didn't even have most of them himself, was unrealistic and demanding. He was going to miss the best woman for him because he was choosing what kind of woman would be perfect for him based on the western Christian mind-set of a perfect 10 woman.

What if the woman is a 5 but her love together makes them both 10's? Of course his ideal woman needed to be attractive to him and love Jesus, but what about the rest? Were his values shallow or deep; were they realistic? He was from a small town, and yet his expectation was to marry a celebrity as opposed to a real woman he might meet at social events. I love unbelievably-high dreams and building a right skeleton based on real desires, but we cannot build our skeletal wish list based on secular values or idealism. (Now might be a good time to go back over your checklist of what you want in a soul mate.)

So when is your *Bambi* springtime? Hopefully, as we continue the process of this book, you will be able to find out!

The Rescuers

If, according to standards you are setting, the person you're into is not a good fit, you might consider dating him/her anyway with the hope that the person may one day become what you desire. You might, as a believer, date people who are not saved, nor do they have any real pursuit of God in their lives. You might meet people who are really immature, but something in you is ready and willing to participate in a relationship with them, even though the better part of you tells you you will not be able to change them. Rescuer types of people do this all the time.

"We forget that marriage is a relationship, not a project to be completed or a problem to solve." Dr. Gary Chapman, *The Five Love Languages*.

Missionary dating

Christians call this type of dating missionary dating because you have to convert the people or persuade them to have a personality or character makeover before they can be fully-healthy individuals (or good enough for you to consider marrying). Doing this gets you into developing the kind of relationships in which you are yoked/tied/bound to others in an unequal way. People let their future happiness depend on other people's choices to live their lives according to the missionary's/rescuer's desires. This is one of the worst methods of dating!

One of my relatives had a problem with missionary dating in her late teens/early twenties. When she was in high school, she was the girl who had the 'it' factor all the guys liked, but the amazing thing about her was that she was a radical Christian. During that time guys would pursue her. She had such a gift of compassion that even though she tried to just keep guys as friends, she would let her heart get overly involved and would end up dating them. The guys would come to church with her, and even go through all the emotions of getting saved. Some even got baptized, but then, as soon as she broke it off with them, the guys would mysteriously disappear—mostly because they were living vicariously through her desire for God. Their desire was really only for her.

Long term

Whenever you are dating others with huge areas of weakness, values that are different, their salvation is in question, etc., with the hopes of changing them, then your little short-term-mission project might become a long-term mission with huge consequences. It is easy to mislead others when you are leading them along, trying to make yourself the environment they can change in; this, my friend, doesn't work long term.

One of my friends said to me, "I would personally consider missionary dating Angelina Jolie if it doesn't work for her and Brad, because I think I could change her." He said this during the time she was being portrayed negatively in the media. Do you hear how ridiculous that sounds, even as a joke? (Ok, ok, it was me . . . I wanted to date Angelina Jolie! I wanted to change her with my real love . . . don't tell anyone)!

Are You Ready To Rumble?

Assuming you now feel like your identity is in God, I've shot down all of your unrealistic idealism, and you no longer have a need to get married but you still want to, it is good to go through a very important heart and thought process next in order to answer this question: **Are you ready to be in a relationship?**

The best things in life are not free. They cost your heart, they cost your time, they cost your money, and they cost a spiritual investment. It's so easy to get all excited about someone without even asking the question, "Am I datable?" When you are interested in pursuing someone or being pursued, you need to ask yourself: "Am I ready to make an investment on all of those levels. Am I healthy in those areas?"

What good is it to want to pursue someone when you are in massive debt and can't afford to date? Or how about pursuing them when you are in school full time and working part time? Are you even datable right now? Or even more serious, is your heart healthy and ready for a relationship? Many relationships start out selfishly because one half of the couple is not really ready to date. In our culture, it is easy to get caught up in attraction and desire instead of being mature about the process, but I am here to help! You can figure out if you are ready to be in a relationship by taking the following test.

Are You Datable?
The 12-Step Self-Evaluation Test

Are you ready?

1. Are you emotionally healthy?

2. How much time do you have to date? Is it enough to just be with someone when you feel like it (which is using them)? Do you really have enough time to give to a relationship?

3. Where are you at spiritually? Are you ready for a relationship? Do you have spiritual relationships with others/a safety net of people set up to help hold you accountable and with whom you can communicate regularly?

4. How is your sex drive? Do you have active lust; are you looking at pornography; are you using the opposite sex for the wrong reasons?

5. What is your loneliness factor, meaning, do you want to date because of loneliness?

6. Have you been in a serious relationship lately, and now that you are single again, do you just want something to fill that void?

7. Are you excited about someone for a balanced set of reasons?

8. Are you bored at all? (The worst relationships start out of boredom.)

9. Are you in more debt than you could pay off in one year (excluding mortgage or school loans)?

10. If you date right now, will it get in the way of education, start-up careers, ministry, or any other areas God might want you to establish before marriage; or are you called to partner with someone in the start up of these things?

11. Most importantly, have you ever had a long period of singleness when you were totally focused on your relationship with God and romance was not in the picture?

12. Is God asking you to set aside a period of time to just pursue Him and have identity in that pursuit, rather than in dating or marriage?

Scoring your survey

I was going to write a scale of scores for this survey, but I didn't want anyone to feel like a loser, so I'm asking you to self-determine how well you did on the survey. If you are a loser, you know you are a loser. God wants to heal you so you can be a winner and either win that bride/bridegroom or live in a fulfilling season with God alone! If you are not a loser, and you are being honest with yourself, are you ready to rumble or do you need development time?

Scoring someone else

If there is someone you are currently interested in, you can go back through the survey and answer the questions as if they were asked about that person. This can help you to determine whether he/she is datable.

What if You're Not Datable?

This will by no means fix you, but I do have some guidelines . . .

Develop the standard: relational skills

Relational skills are learned behavior, and social intelligence is not natural for most people. Sure, you know how to be polite (most of the time); you can relate to people you have natural chemistry with also, on a certain level, but the deeper you want to go in a relationship, the more work it takes. That means part of developing your standards is growing in your skill of being able to relate to people.

How do you do this realistically? I think you (and everyone else) have a responsibility to find balanced relationships, or materials on them, and find out how you rate next to them. Then go on a journey to become balanced. If you come from a broken home, what areas do you need to grow in to know how to be a part of a functional family? If you have failed in many dating situations, how can you grow in ways that will help you relate to others in a deeper way? Do you need counseling? Do you need a life coach? Are you willing to pay a price and spend some time to develop skills that are foreign to you? Common relational skills that are the most underdeveloped in people are:

- ☐ Conflict management
- ☐ Building a true foundation of trust
- ☐ Learning to affirm another person in the way that relates to him/her the most
- ☐ Communicating deliberately about what God is doing in your life and sharing it with another person so he/she can be included in the process

These are all important areas that, many times, get little or no attention.

Understand the opposite sex

Have you ever evaluated how you relate to those of the opposite sex according to their possible point of view? How well do you treat them in their estimation, not your own? I believe many people fail in relationships because they put out signals that they don't understand the opposite sex in the first place. I have one friend who treats girls like they are guys, so girls only see him as a big brother. (You can only burp in a girl's face once before she puts you into another category.) He is lonely and wants marriage, but he doesn't know how to love and honor a female's womanliness.

I have a girl friend who just can't relate to guys' humor, desire for sports, etc., but she wants a manly man, not a metrosexual. Her problem is she always talks badly about true men because of her lack of understanding, so they just avoid her. She has great shopping partners, though . . .

Understanding the opposite sex's motivations, desires, and even patterns can help you to seem more appealing to them. The more understanding you have, the more relatable you will be to the opposite sex. If you are going to set some standards on how you treat members of the opposite sex, you have to understand them, not just according to those in your family or friendship network, but in general.

See and love your value. Learn how to send the signal

Some religious cultures have such a no-flirting policy that they raise girls and guys in a bubble of religion that sometimes neuters their sex appeal. Because of it, many guys and girls in the church don't allow themselves to be attractive. Just because most sex appeal crosses over to seduction or lust, this doesn't mean we can't find a place of balance. God gives us the ability to be cute to those of the opposite sex when we are interested in them; there is definitely an innate ability to send out a signal when we like someone.

Sex appeal is natural to every kind of animal; it is the sending of signals to someone you like. This is proven in nature, it's proven psychologically, and it's proven in advertising, but sending out signals to someone we are interested in can only come naturally if we are in touch with our own desirability.

I know one girl who hasn't had any guy pursue her in about fifteen years, but she is beautiful. She doesn't come off as attractive, though. She always complains that no one comes after her and that she hasn't dated in a coon's age.

The thing is, when men in her age group come around her, there is nothing that she does to make herself available. She comes across as a sister or mother, not as an available woman. They have no clue that she exists on a romantic relational level, and part of it is because she doesn't seem to present herself as a romantic equivalent. She knows she is naturally pretty; she has been told she is over and over again, but she doesn't enjoy her own beauty. One time I saw her try, and it was embarrassing for her. Her efforts looked like the shameless flirting of a five year old who had a crush—because she was so out of touch with her own appeal.

Everything can change for this girl once she chooses to get in touch with her beauty and worth, and she starts investing in it. In other words, if she allows herself to feel beautiful and get the healing she needs (to learn how to operate out of that internal beauty) she will start to send the right signals outwardly.

You have to love yourself. There are three primary commandments in the Bible: Love God, love your neighbor, and love yourself (God's creation). If you don't know your own value, you will not know how to present that value and worth to others. It's so important to value your personality, your character, and your uniqueness. Once you know that:

- ☐ You are God's masterpiece
- ☐ There is no one else exactly like you for a reason
- ☐ God has given you exactly what you need to complement others
- ☐ Everything about you has value

When you know that you are offering something of value to those around you and they can perceive your value. This is greater than sex appeal alone, and it comes across in all your interactions with other people.

In all your social exchanges, you give from your wealth of personality, character, and spiritual strength. If all of these things are invisible to you, they will be invisible to others too. You will not send out healthy vibrations of affection for others if you have no affection for yourself.

Match made in heaven, if they weren't invisible to each other

Darlene, one of our better friends, hadn't been asked out in over a decade. She is an awesome person, full of grace, and pretty, yet it seemed as if no one knew she existed on a relational level. We also have another invisible friend, Kevin. He has an amazing career, a runner's body, a great smile, and a sweet personality. He had not dated in over ten years either, and he was sick of being alone. Darlene and Kevin had known each other for at least five years, but as I said, they were invisible to everyone on a relational level, even to themselves.

One day, as they were sitting next to each other at a group meeting at my house, the light went on in my head that they could like each other, and on some level did . . . they just weren't in touch with their own feelings! I talked to them individually and found out they were both completely open to the idea. They'd even had little minor what if thoughts about each other before! Their first date went splendidly, and I guess the rest did too, because now they are married and have a family! (I should add the title "Matchmaker" to the many titles on my business card.)

So why, when they had feelings for each other, did they not send out a signal? Why was there no communication about their feelings? Because they weren't in touch with themselves, with their emotions, and with their own value.

The
Preemtive
Guide

The Moral Compass

We talked in previous chapters about setting some standards in your friendship and dating relationships, but you cannot do that if you do not develop your own moral compass *before* you date anyone. Others cannot be your moral compass for you, even when you try and let them run the ship.

I have a personal exercise trainer, and I tried to put pressure on the poor guy to be my motivator. It worked while he was at the gym with us. (It's so easy to put that role on others and then live vicariously through their drives and passions.) This seemed to work until certain moments would hit, like . . . the late-night munchies would hit me and the peanut butter M&M demon would visit. I couldn't call my motivator in the middle of the night (or, at least, he wouldn't answer, because I tried); I had to have a personal foundation of principles to give me the motivation to throw away that chunky monkey ice cream that so loves my midsection.

You will not be motivated to follow your moral compass unless you value the health of your whole being. The reality is that most people feel ready for a relationship right now, but they haven't done the foundational work on themselves to be qualified for one. I don't want to be idealistic, you will never be ready for marriage if it's about perfection, and we all know that; but you do have a responsibility to be as healthy as possible by having a basic foundation in place. Each person who goes on the journey of marriage will get extremely strengthened through it, which proves we have a lot of weak areas before marriage, but what are you doing to strengthen yourself right now? What is your growth plan? What are your core values?

When you focus on building a moral compass inside your soul and you stick to the plan, even when you are swayed by your emotions, your will will have no choice but to override the emotions.

Sometimes words like "holiness" and "purity" can be so obscure—people can have very strange or self-serving or unrealistic definitions for them. Basically, having holiness or the fear of God means you will do anything you can to protect your relationship with Him. For example: A man who loves his marriage of twenty-five years does not give into a sexual feeling he has for a woman walking by; he loves his wife too much. He protects the quality of his connection by not giving into a one-night-stand.

Why do we not have affairs or wrong boundaries with the opposite sex? Because we are trying to keep our hearts healthy; we are determined to protect the relationships we love and have sacrificed so much for!

What makes up the moral compass?

Recipe
- ☐ High standards
- ☐ Basic moral values
- ☐ A fine dose of character

Instructions
Mix high standards with basic moral values and add a seasoned dash of a fine dose of character. Bake until cemented in the mind.

When your moral compass works, it tells you to run away from your attraction to someone who does not qualify as being datable. (Maybe he/she has rage issues or other problems.) Your moral compass says, "He/she is not worth it!" because your value system is doing its job. It enforces your self-respect, core values, and high standards to be with someone who is relationally whole, and who is a good fit for you.

IIf your moral compass is broken, though, you can find yourself getting into a relationship that takes the wind right out of your sails. I know one fine specimen of Christianity who became attracted to a girl who joined his worship team. She presented herself a certain way, but everyone around this young man knew she had issues. His parents, who are amazing people, warned him; his worship team warned him, and his friends even complained about her because she was very controlling and manipulative. He decided to go with his own compass, which had a new pointer based in his pants (not based on values), and he dated the girl for a while.

During that time, she drove a wedge between him and every other relationship he had. She controlled him in almost every way. One day, after tons of drama and unhappiness, he woke up from his stupor and realized he was not following his moral compass. Actually, he thought he had gotten her pregnant, but it was a false alarm. He could see she was the only one left in his life, and they were making bad choices together.

She was so angry and unexciting that he was missing what life was all about . . . community. He had no more community. She was so broken she was scared to be involved with other people. He left because she refused to change, and he went back to the community and family he had isolated himself from. Luckily, love covers a multitude of failures.

Relational morality

Morality is a tough issue to understand or follow, especially because each denomination preaches a different moral interpretation of how to live life. We are not talking about the basics like, *"just say no to sex!"* Morality is more about the development of your conscience or inner voice of reason. It's the little angel on your shoulder who speaks words of wisdom to you. It's the moral compass that doesn't just point north, south, east and west; it points to life, death, right, and wrong too.

Your moral compass can not only tell you what the right choice is, in a given situation; it can also tell you which actions will bring health to you (and others) and which ones will cut off relationships. Your words and the attitude of your heart have this kind of power. Let's put it this way: you can win a game of Russian roulette and still die. It's not always about winning and being right when someone's life is on the line.

If your girlfriend asks you, after she got the worst haircut of her life, if she still looks pretty to you, do you give her the black-and-white answer? Or do you look at her and choose to bring her life and not death? This means you take into consideration what is in her heart. We are not talking about being deceptive. What if you love your girlfriend, and she is pretty to you but you don't like her haircut? Can you be constructive and real but also sensitive enough to build her up, not tear her down? Maybe you say she is always beautiful and you love when she tries something new, but this isn't your favorite. Maybe you aren't qualified to judge style, so you just say you love her and that she is attractive. There are so many other choices than, "You're so ugly, that ain't a hair line it's your hair running away from your face!"

My young friend Justin (probably not his real name) was hitting on a girl, but because of his lack of understanding of women, he was coming across as a total jerk. She rejected him and told him he was a jerk. He came over, defeated, and asked me, "Was I being a jerk?" In that moment of vulnerability, my moral compass had to guide me, because if it was just a black-and-white question I might have said something like, "Jerk may not be the word she was thinking, you were actually a _____."

But the reality is that just to agree and be condescending, even if I was right about my opinion, wouldn't help him grow. That would be a right-and-wrong perspective. He had honestly asked for my viewpoint. The better thing for ol' Justin (probably still not his name) was to give him the truth in the most constructive, conditioned-with-love way I could. This doesn't mean I would give false language or a positive spin. If I was going to help build Justin's life and not bring death to his personality, his ego, and his heart, then I needed to be patient but real. Yes, he came across wrong, but I know him and he has a good heart. He's just maturing. So I said to Justin, "You didn't show her who you were in your interaction; you made her feel you were only trying to get a date with her. You need to show her who you are and why you care about her instead of trying to just operate out of chemistry." I would hope this imaginary Justin would return the favor.

Physical morality

Having a complete grasp of relational morality means you have to decide what is wrong and right when setting your physical boundaries. It is so important, once you are getting close enough to where physical things are happening naturally, to have a talk, otherwise you might get into the everything-but-intercourse mode of operating. Those who don't lead a discussion will lead by their instincts, and instincts can be very deceptive, if not sensual. So many people have never been told to have regular talks about physical boundaries, but once you have begun a healthy relationship and you are organically starting the physical process, talking about physical boundaries is essential. The problem is, too much talk ruins the mood of romance and can break apart what is organic and natural, but too little talk leads to too much of a physically-romantic mood. If your relationships are going to keep developing within your pre-chosen moral boundaries and you want them to stay balanced, you need to have talks beforehand *and* debriefing talks at times.

If I were to make an educated guess on who would be naturally willing to have these talks, it would probably be those who had open sex and boundaries talks with their parents. It is a *huge* problem if you, as a parent, can't talk to your kids because you have made talking about sex awkward and uneasy. If you cannot talk directly about setting boundaries, but instead hint and try to drop them clues, your kids will have a hard time talking to their partners about the same things.

Developing a moral compass and maintaining moral boundaries are dependant on healthy communication. You need to fight selfish desires to get involved on a physical level just because you want to enjoy sexual activities outside of marriage. Most of the times you get involved physically (beyond innocent kisses or hugs), the relationship turns into a taking of each other instead of the mutual sharing of a moment. Many people don't realize how selfish this is until after they break up and then they feel like they have been stolen from.

Each time you leave a relationship you can do an evaluation of how close you stayed to your moral compass. Don't use introspection here; just be honest with yourself so you can set even better, if not higher, standards the next time.

Compass-setting time

1. What do I feel is ok to do physically in a relationship?

2. What do I feel is crossing the line?

3. Do I have control of my current sexual desires?

4. On a scale from 1-10:

☐ I often initiate physical touch.
☐ I have consistently been the one to take touch to the next level.
☐ I have had a good moral compass.
☐ I have had sexual experiences that I am confused about.
☐ I am comfortable with having no sexual contact, until marriage, with the person I am dating.

She Touched My Special Place!
Restoring the Past before You Disrupt the Future

There is something really amazing about walking in purity. I love being clean (actually, I love to get muddy and all outdoorsy, but that's a totally different subject). Most people who are in the Church know enough to have to be pure but they don't always know enough to *want* to be pure.

If you ask the average church person why they don't have sex outside of marriage, their answer would be, "Because it's a sin." This is a very simplistic and often non-empowering way to look at it. If the only goal of not engaging in sexual activity outside of marriage is to not sin, then we are doomed—our flesh will always tempt us with excuses and give us reasons why we can violate our own principles for the sake of pleasure.

These choices have to be made from a marriage of right thinking (aka good theology) and a healthy heart choice. My belief is that you can not make consistently good choices with either theology or heart relationship alone, but if you have both, then you will keep on making spiritually-motivated (a combination of the Word and the Spirit at work within you) decisions.

The motivator for purity is fulfillment in relationships

If we look at the subject of sex from an eternal perspective, God doesn't tell us to not have sex without commitment just so we'll be pure; He wants us to be pure for the sake of fullness in our intimate lives with Him and our spouses. In other words, becoming one and maintaining oneness with someone, and connecting on the deepest level of union and understanding with that person, is His gift to us—fulfillment beyond measure.

You were born a sexual creature. If you didn't think so when you were younger, by the time God hit the puberty button in your body you figured it out. If you grew up in church, you had messages of purity and abstinence preached at you for most of your life. I don't want to develop chapters and chapters on basic Christian morality because there are excellent books on this, but let's go over the basics:

1. You are only supposed to enter into a sexual relationship with your spouse (spouse meaning person of the opposite sex).

2. Anything you do that stimulates the other person sexually instantly puts you into a sexual relationship. The Bible is not *just* addressing the actual act of copulation (that word is so scientific, and this is probably the only time I have ever used it); it's addressing everything that is sexual.

3. When dating, this means you should not do anything to stimulate your date sexually. This includes kissing in sensual ways, petting, touching, prodding, lifting, scratching, breathing, snorting, oogling, tickling, cooing, etc, with any part of your body that stimulates you *or* your partner into a sexual relationship. It also includes anything you are enticed to take a piece of clothing off for.

Soul ties are sticky

When people cross the line of purity with a person of the opposite sex, they give a part of themselves away that sticks to the other person forever. That part can only be given back to them, or taken back, through prayer and repentance. You may not realize how powerful sexuality is, but every time you cross the line and engage in intimacy and sexual activity with someone, you open yourself up to become a part of everything in that person.

Think about King David. He gave part of himself to Bathsheba. He knew it was wrong, but at the same time that his moral compass was shutting down, David had her husband killed so that he could be the sole possessor of Bathsheba's affections. He had a tie to her that went beyond reason, beyond normal affection; his tie to her made him begin to act irrationally. This is not the only time the Bible demonstrates the loss of a brain because of a very sexual relationship that lay way outside the boundaries of a person's moral compass.

In marriage, a sexual relationship helps a couple to unite in God's purest way—two people give themselves in a selfless act of love; they consummate their union over and over (and if you are healthy, over and over again). It goes beyond what is naturally stimulating. The act of sex bonds the couple in a way which cannot be uttered in words; it is a bond which cannot be gotten any other way; it creates/continues the highest bond of friendship and relationship possible between two people. Sexual intimacy was designed to create a spiritual bond that would enable two people to truly know each other. That's why many biblical translations of the word for sex would be translated like this: "Abraham knew Sarah." This meant Abraham had sexual intimacy with Sarah, in effect, knowing her in the highest-possible way.

When you begin to satisfy your spouse sexually, you add the unique functions of sexual intimacy (trust, play, sharing, security, and sacrifice) to your foundation. Obviously, it is just one part of a healthy relationship. It *helps* build the foundation in a marriage, even if it is *not* the foundation itself.

Sexual relationships outside of marriage

If you begin to have sexual intimacy without marriage, it's like the two of you open a dual credit card in the spirit. The other person's emotional issues and spiritual junk, aka the debt, becomes your debt, and the interest can be terrible! No matter whom the other person ends up accruing more debt with, you are stuck with all the sexual history and spiritual debt of his/her life up to the point when you two were intimate. Another way of saying this is: sexually transmitted diseases are not the only infections you can get from sexual intimacy—the bondage, sin patterns, and brokenness which belong to the other person can now belong to you.

One young man, who we'll call John, who I had always known as being very masculine and straight, slept with a girl who was into bisexuality. After he broke it off with her, he began to struggle with homosexual thoughts, even though he had never engaged directly in any of her fantasies. It's as if they had a Vulcan mind meld (reference from *Star Trek*: the two became one). Although he didn't give himself over to a homosexual lifestyle, and he obviously wasn't a homosexual, these thoughts broke out like a chronic rash after being with her. That's pretty amazing in principle: if I engage someone sexually, I can be embedded with their emotional, spiritual, and mental bondage.

We prayed for him, he had a little counseling, and he broke off any ties to her which he had made. Many of you have heard of soul ties: they happen when two people give themselves to inappropriate intimacy and their souls are tied together. There can be transference either way. Soul ties can curse our lives, be leeches to our emotions and strength, and keep us committing to relationships we don't even really want to be in.

Soul ties don't just happen when two people have a sexual relationship, either. They can happen when:

- ☐ We start to have inappropriate affections for someone
- ☐ We give our hearts away to someone, isolating ourselves from other influences
- ☐ We go too fast in building a relationship with another, and the foundation of our relationship is not strong enough to handle our dependence on him/her
- ☐ We are in a time of great need and we let one person fill all of our emotional or spiritual needs, instead of spreading our needs out to our community of friendships and to God

In other words, soul ties can happen for many reasons.

She couldn't get away because he owned her

I had a friend, let's call her Martha, who began to enter into a sexually-stimulating relationship. The couple never committed the act of sex, but they did many other things to stimulate each other. When Martha's boy-friend began to grow complacent and lazy, she stayed hooked into the dead-end relationship because she was bonded to him, tied to him, and she revolved her life around him. Through her sexual experiences with him, she had opened a door to an addiction to him similar to a crack addict's to his pipes. This door not only made them more dependent on each other; it was literally stealing Martha's life from her.

Martha could not be truly happy with the relationship, and she could not be happy with someone who would not enter into the true purpose of a sexual relationship with her (marital union). He didn't have to make a real commitment to the relationship because Martha was giving him everything he wanted. He had pleasure without consequence. He could leave her at any time, for days at a time, and then come back to her on his terms.

She couldn't break it off with him until we prayed. Through the prayer, she took back everything she had given him, and she gave him back everything he had given her. Once that was done, it was as if her eyes opened. She seemed to suddenly wonder what in the heck she was doing with him.

Martha walked away from him and never looked back. It's not always that easy, but it is that real.

Restoration of virginity

What is virginity? It's the state of being free and pure—physically, spiritually, and emotionally. Virgins are people who have not given themselves to anyone; no one has ownership over them, either sexually or relationally. Being a virgin is not just about being someone who hasn't had sex. It's about being someone who walks in line with purity, being someone who has not given parts of him/her self away.

God can restore you to a state of virginity by taking back ownership of the pieces you have given away, as well as releasing you from the emotional marks of those experiences. He can also send back the pieces of the other person you have taken. To be a virgin means to be sexually unhitched from every other human being, and to be fully pure in your heart and in your devotion to God. Your soul is free, your mind is free, and your heart is free to be one with God again. This is much more important virginity than just the physical fact that you have not had sex. We jokingly call it being a "born-again virgin."

As a matter of fact, you can be a virgin again, although it's not like an old-time-religion altar call when you can come and get resaved every time you feel bad. We are talking about the principle of what it is to walk with God, unshackled from bad choices and wrong soul ties.

Ripping apart the soul ties

Throughout the years, I have loved to watch God completely unshackle people from their ties of bondage to past sexual and romantic relationships. He heals hearts and minds completely by dealing with the roots of the relationships.

One of our friends had had sexual relationships with so many people that, as we prayed for him, we could hear a ripping or tearing-out sound, as if God was pulling those relationships out by their roots. The guy was never the same.

God wants you to be a virgin in your mind, heart, and spirit. He wants your mind to be renewed to a place of purity, your heart to be restored to a place of emotional health, and your spirit to be free from the false connections from the past. In the cross, there is provision for you to be completely restored.

Prayer for calling it all back and restoring purity

If you have had (one or more) sexual relationships, you need God to give you back what you gave away, and you also need Him to send back what you took. Start by praying about it. Here is a simple prayer which can start this journey for you:

Jesus,

I am sorry for giving myself to another person (other people) in these ways, and I understand why it was wrong.

Please send back what I took from that person (those people) I committed these acts with.

Please wash me from any effects of the bondage he/she/they were controlled by, the fruit of the wrong choices he/she/they made, and the sinful patterns he/she/they had.

I give back the places I touched, the fantasy life I had, and the purity I stole.

In turn, please give back to me what I gave him/her/them——it was meant to be yours first and then my spouse's.

Please touch my mind and cleanse it from the memories of what we did together.

Please wash away my body's physical memories and its sexually-awakened urges.

Please don't allow sexual dreams or reenactments of these situations and cleanse me from them.

I take back every body part I gave and allowed him/her/them to use in a wrong way.

I cut any tie that was attached to him/her/them because of these deeds, in your name, Jesus.

I release him/her/them completely from his/her/their connection or tie to me via these acts.

I release him/her/them to be his/her/their own person.

Please bless those I failed with.

Please help me to make wise decisions with my sexual desires.

Help me to be restored to a virgin state in my spirit, soul, and heart.

Teach me how to have my first and main union with you (that my whole being desires) so when I do get married, I will know how to fully give myself to the one I love.

Amen.

The good news

The good news is that even if you are in a relationship with someone who you plan on marrying, but you have failed with them on a moral level, you can have relational restoration. There is a process, though, of putting up good physical boundaries for the sake of walking in His fullness, not just for the sake of avoiding sin. As your heart connects back to Jesus' heart of love, I pray you will be able to make the right decisions, for His sake.

So You Like Her

What Now?

Your hands are all sweaty and your heart is beating uncontrollably! Your tongue is swollen and you have pitted out your shirt, all because there is someone around you that you like, and you believe she may like you too!

Ok, ok, you may have never felt this way since junior high, but I have still had my magic chemistry moments when I puffed my chest up, pulled my shoulders back, cocked my head right, and walked over to talk to that special someone.

So what do you do when you feel qualified and datable, and you meet the right qualified and datable person? It's different for everyone. There is no magic formula for the pursuit, but the exciting thing is that you *can* pursue him/her!

The One and Only Stalkers Chapter

But . . . before you pursue someone, I want to delve into an incredibly deceptive attitude which has, unfortunately, influenced many people of all ages in the church. You knew it would come: the one and only chapter on Christian stalkers. This isn't a "how to be a Christian stalker," though. I wanted to write that but I didn't have enough experience.

I am just going to tell a few stories, because sometimes a story is worth a thousand sermons. I didn't want to put pictures in (like one of the woman who showed up to one of my events in a wedding dress, wanting to marry me right then and there; or the stalker with the restraining order against her who dressed up like Tina Turner to sneak into our meeting so she could confront me with her love . . . great pictures, but for obvious reasons they will remain out of this). I didn't want to add anything visual to this because it could get scary.

If you are being stalked, please talk to your leadership in your church, and if it's serious, then talk to the police. I have had to do both. If you are stalking someone, stop it. Falling in love is a relational process, not an exclusive pursuit of obsession.

Don't you just adore how many people mistake their inner voices of obsession for God's words of love . . . ?

Does that mean God sounds crazy to many people?

Sometimes the voice people hear is obviously demonic, or even plain insane, but sometimes people just want something so badly they deceive themselves for the sake of misguided love.

That was the case of Angelina (changed name for the book for obvious reasons, and I like that name, it will help me to write this). I was in a city praying for everyone in the church, and when I went to the back row, there was Angelina. She was very excited when I got to her, although I didn't notice how much so. When the meeting was over, I could tell she wanted to connect, which happens often on trips. I didn't have time, so I did a minister's avoidance walk (walk very fast, holding your cell phone or some other such object, and try to look busy and important so people will leave you alone).

Years went by, and since I barely noticed her, I didn't notice at all when she moved to my city. Little did I know that the night I had prayed for her, the girl and her whole church thought she heard from God that I was *The One*! She began to get involved with people who were close to my friends, and pretty soon she was hanging out around us regularly. I just thought that, out of kindness, the guys and girls were reaching out to someone who had a huge rejection issue. I accepted that, but I avoided her for the most part because I felt a weird vibe from her.

In her mind her plan was working, and she was actually setting goals to become friends with my family, my friends, my dog and, ultimately, me. She then moved a block away, which in our town was noticeable. I would often see her car drive down our street, instead of hers, to get home. Then I started running into her at restaurants, grocery stores, and other public places. As a matter of fact, when I would arrive at church, she would mysteriously be there at the same time. I was starting to get creeped out. I asked one of our friends who seemed to know her the best if she had a job, and she didn't. She literally showed up where I was at least once a day, if not everywhere I went, and would say, "Wow, this is amazing! We must be destined to see each other." *No, creepy lady, it was you following me here in a very strange way so you could pursue your fantasy life.*

This began her full-time stalking of me. I asked our mutual friend to talk to her about backing off because it was getting weird. That's when I received a twelve-page hand-written letter that smelled of some biblical fragrance that basically said she was praying for me to know I was to be her husband, and if I didn't marry her by a certain date, I would die. Yes, you heard it right. She said that she knew as soon as I came all the way to the back of her church just to pray for her. I was shocked, because that night I prayed for literally everyone in the church. I had not made a special point to pray for just her, as she had perceived. She also talked about demons that had been plaguing her ever since, trying to get her to deny the fact she had heard from God about me. (I wonder if those were angels of mercy.)

I went to my leaders, and they talked to her. They asked her, "Are you open to the fact that you may be deceived in this?" She said no, and again mentioned my death in a letter. When I showed it to the police, they believed it was a death threat. I had to get a restraining order. She was really interestingly sweet (although strange and eccentric) in person, but the letters that came in were getting darker and darker, telling me she was God's agent assigned to destroy me if I didn't fulfill the promise. Finally she had a breakdown and got medication and stopped.

Facebook

My second story is about a woman who I'd accepted as a friend on my Facebook account. She'd believed for quite some time that I was going to be her husband. She looked at my pictures and profile dozens of times a day. I didn't know who she was among my thousands of friends on there. She began to anonymously write long love letters to me, in a program that let's you do that. I had to delete the program. She tried for four years to write any way she could. Then she sent a letter stating she was coming to the airport, and I needed to pick her up so we could fall in love with each other. It was very strange. One of my team had to respond to her and confront her. She admitted to getting into deception. I believe she will have a fulfilled life, since she can move on now.

Secret fantasy life

Another stalker I had was very intense. She got very close to my whole friendship network. I had known her for quite some time, but she was like a little sister in a way. I didn't know she had made up a whole fantasy life about our marriage and the kids we would have. After not seeing her for close to a year, her parents' friends asked for an emergency meeting one night and I didn't know why. They met with me to confront me on why I was not committing to her. I had no idea what they were talking about. They said that when we had been on our date the night before, I had talked about marriage, and they wondered why I was leading her on without commitment. I told them I was out with friends the night before and I hadn't seen her in over a year, and I didn't know what they were talking about. I told them I had never dated her, secretly or publicly.

That's when they told me her story. She would actually disappear from her house, telling everyone she was dating me and they had to keep it a secret. She'd made up a secret life, and would talk about me to her close and extended family structure all the time. She would tell them what I had said and what I liked. It was very sad because I hadn't talked to her at all, about anything, and yet she felt the need to validate her fantasy life of marriage to me by lying to her family. She even had a secret prayer list for our marriage among her friends, and claimed to travel and minister with me! She may have had a mental disorder, but she probably just chose to believe a lie (which was scary enough). Luckily, her family intervened.

The Korean Esther

Last one. My last stalker story is the saddest and most ridiculous one. I do not feel bad about talking about it publically because we made such an effort to communicate with the girl's pastors and friends about the deception this woman was in. We even talked with her face-to-face many times. She is still obsessed with me to this day.

I was speaking in one of the many wonderful churches in Korea, and at the end I prayed a release for women who felt they had passion like that of Esther (of the Bible). I prayed with the pastors with each of the women, and there were hundreds.

One of these women had received a prophecy from another Korean that she was about to meet her husband and that he was going to pray a release of an Esther promise over her. Well, in comes Shawn, who innocently prays over a whole room of women, one by one. This woman was hooked from the moment I prayed for her. She even went so far as to change her name to Esther because she believed I wanted to marry a woman called Esther.

This began a violently-intrusive stalking period during which she began to get as close to me from another foreign country as she could. She called some twenty times a day on multiple ministry phone numbers. She tried to send gifts. Whenever I visited Korea she was in every meeting, and would sit as high as she could so I would notice her. If I did notice her, she would lip the words *I love you* and draw circles around her heart. She even got to the point where she showed up at the airport for a few days to wait for me because she didn't know when I would leave. She wanted to go home with me and said she was ready to be married.

I told her I was not going to be her husband and she needed to give up this fantasy. I was very kind, but direct. I then asked many of my dear Korean friends (pastors) to talk to her about it, and they came back and told me her response. She said, "Shawn made such harsh statements because he was testing my devotion to him. I know now, more than ever, that I am to marry him!"

She began to order all my teaching CDs from churches or conferences I went to, and she would use any information she could to find out where I would be or what I was doing. She went to Los Angeles a few weeks before I moved there and told the LAPD I was her fiancé and had abandoned her. Angry, they called me. Naturally, I told them I didn't even know her. She broke into houses of people who had the same names as team members of Expression58 just to get my phone number out of their address books (which wasn't there because she went to the wrong houses). She went to jail over ten times. Even after all of this, she began to show up at my meetings. We had to have her arrested many times. She would show up in wedding dresses, holding notes or gifts, demanding time with me and demanding to go home with me. She tried to bribe me by offering me four million American dollars to get married. I was tempted . . . just kidding!

A year went by. We hadn't heard from her, so I felt great. It was a huge relief to think it was over, but . . . a birthday package arrived for me which had no name of sender. I opened it right on the front row at the beginning of my church service. (I have never opened packages there before, but I had several birthday presents around me.) In it were a wedding-photo frame and a small box. The box had some tighty-whitey underwear which was hysterically obscene, and the note in the box was from Esther, in which she asked me to take a photo wearing the underwear, frame it, and send it to her!

This shows you how someone's deception and fantasy life can cause distraction, crime, and even endanger lives.

Stalkers "R" Us

What gets someone to the point of deception that these girls had gotten to? (And many of my single girlfriends have had male stalkers.) How do you believe in something so much that you will lie to yourself and live a fantasy? I can't tell you, but what I do know is that stalking starts with believing a lie. These are only a few of about twelve stories, and I am not telling you the most dangerous or bizarre ones.

I am only telling you my end of these stories as a male victim, but this happens both ways. In a psychology magazine I read a few years ago, it said men are more prone to stalk than women. These stories are even more frightening because men are more aggressive pursuers. I have not done research on it, but it makes sense.

I don't want to comment much on what I am writing other than this: If you know someone has a revelation or a desire to marry you (not to date or get to know you), please respond immediately. Bring someone with you and tell them directly that you are not interested in marrying them. They need to have the opportunity to hear the truth. This way, you can (hopefully) stop things during the more innocent early days of attraction, long before it can turn into fully-fledged stalking.

I also want to note that many girls who write me e-mails always qualify it by saying they don't want to be taken as one of my stalkers. These make me laugh, but it is also sad. Please don't qualify yourselves to me; I trust that 99 percent of women are innocent. The real stalkers are obvious and scary. You are innocent until proven guilty. I know most girls are not writing to get me to be their husband. I love friendship.

So . . . now that we know you are not stalker material, what's your next move?

Some Helpful
Pick Up Lines (not)

Are you a parking ticket?
[What?]
You got fine written all over you.

Can I borrow a quarter?
[What for?]
I want to call my mom and tell her I just met the girl of my dreams.

When I saw you from across the room, I passed out cold and hit my head on the floor . . . so I'm going to need your name and number for insurance reasons.

Did you have Campbell's soup today?
[No, why?]
Because you're lookin' mmm, mmm good!

Excuse me, but do you have tickets?
[Tickets for what?]
(Point to arm and flex)
To the gun show!

I'm invisible.
[Really?]
Can you see me?
[Yes]
How about tomorrow night?

Giant polar bear
[What?]
It broke the ice.

Barbed Wire Boundaries

Congratulations! You've had your first date and you had a blast! You want to see much, much, more of him/her, but you're a bit nervous about not screwing it all up.

Have you ever seen that tattoo with the heart that has barbed wire circled around it? That is what we are going to attempt to do together here. So how do you set boundaries that keep your heart safe? How about keeping a potential date safe from your own weaknesses? This chapter is all about defining immovable lines of demarcation in the relationship so you can have the healthiest relationship possible. Some of the things I say will be repeats, but bear with me.

Barbed wire boundary 1: Time management

When you're dating it's so much fun to just hang out, and keep hanging out, and then pretty soon, that's all a couple does all day (and sometimes into the wee hours of the morning). When you get into a relationship, it is so important to set boundaries on how the two of you are going to spend your time. You just need some simple planning and time management so that when it's midnight, and you are cuddling on a couch all alone together, not doing anything except watching a little TV, and the old movie *Top Gun* comes on and the "Take My Breath Away" scene shows, you will change the channel and not reenact it.

A *huge* key to successfully dating and staying out of trouble is the setting of boundaries. Together you need to decide:

- ☐ How much time you will spend together
- ☐ How you will manage your schedules
- ☐ Which kinds of activities you will do
- ☐ How late you will stay at each other's place

Nearly all guys are most vulnerable when they are tired and lacking goals. This happens for me after about midnight. If I were dating, I would just like to sit close on a couch and talk; but if you are alone together, this can turn into lying on the couch . . . and then a cute kiss . . . and then . . . oops, there it is! I think when you get into a dating relationship, you have to decide together what a healthy amount of time to spend in each other's company looks like and agree to not compromise on that.

It is also good to ask some of the friends and authority figures you are involved with how they perceive your relationship. Do they see it as all consuming or balanced? Their perceptions are huge when planning how much time you'll be spending together.

When you begin to compromise and spend too much time (like every waking hour) together, you are crossing a line between what is healthy and what is not, because it means you are isolating yourselves from other relationships. People who spend this amount of time together are almost always also neglecting their relationship with God. That means they are sacrificing Jesus at the altar of worldly romance, not to mention their other friendships. This leads us to number two.

Barbed wire boundary 2: Keeping other friendships intact

Most guys who fail in relationships, whether physically or emotionally, have one major thing in common: they isolate themselves from the rest of their friends and spend all their time with their new gal pal. This is one of the most unhealthy ways to build a relationship, because not only do you end up codependent with the person you are dating, you have no one else to process life with in a regular way, and your perspective can begin to get very warped and self-serving. I don't know how many people I know who have lost great God-given relationships to their dating selfishness. Your friendships may change as you begin to get involved in a more serious dating relationship, but your core-life friendships shouldn't stop. They should evolve with you, and only very rarely should the lifelong godly friendships go away.

An old model from one stream of the Church does try and tell you to die to all friendships for the sake of your new love, but this is not only unbiblical, it is an anti-christ message. As a Christian, you are dependant on the community God is raising up around you, not just on the new relationship you are pursuing. Even if this person is *The One*, it takes a village to raise a child; it takes everyone in your life to keep you balanced.

Barbed wire boundary 3: Setting physical boundaries early

Most people set physical boundaries when it is too late, especially in Christian circles. It's easy to say, *"We will not have sex!"* but it's hard to define the other physical stuff, and many couples just end up crossing everything off the list. Usually the best time to set the minor physical boundaries in place is after the first date, or maybe at the end of the second. Sometimes girls find it's time to set the boundaries when the guy moves in for a kiss good night (or, if he is polite, asks for one). Sometimes, for the guys, it's when the girl runs over and sits on the guy's lap while they are hanging out. The important thing is to set boundaries, even if it's in response to a physical reaction or pursuit either of you are making. When you set a boundary, like saying you do not want to kiss, and the other person tries to kiss you anyway, it is a good sign that the relationship doesn't have a good foundation of respect and honor and it's time to leave it behind. If you are the one trying to move the boundary, you'd better begin to talk before you begin to act.

I know many young people who begin kissing and it gets a little out of hand. Instead of getting ashamed and avoiding communication, it is best to communicate about what just happened so you can be clear, not just on setting up boundaries, but also so you don't start a cycle of shame that often causes the relationship to feel oppressive. Just be open with each other and repent. Also, stay accountable by opening up to somebody you trust in a one-on-one setting. Get some advice if it happens more than once, because when you stop honoring your own boundaries, it will cause resentment, shame, or guilt; and every relationship born with these at play ends up in problems.

Barbed wire boundary 4: Building boundaries based on strengths and weaknesses

If you have had sexual contact or imbalanced relationships, be real about them and then get healing for them, fast. Get someone with maturity to walk through your past choices with you so you can figure out what happened, why they happened, and how you will do relationships next time. You will have a tendency to repeat past failures, no matter how good you feel now. Every time you cross a line, it creates a pattern in your flesh that your flesh remembers and wants to recreate (substitute penis for flesh if you are thinking right about this). It's like muscle memory in a workout. Just being accountable and talking about these things is usually not enough; it's good to find out how you got there, and then also go through self-forgiveness and forgiveness for the one you went there with.

I know that many religious groups/churches kill their wounded, especially when it comes to sexual misconduct—if you admit weakness, you will be looked down upon or disqualified. This is one of the main reasons why so many people don't just fail, but live in failure. You need help when you feel like you have failed, and there are safe people who can help you.

Barbed wire boundary 5: Not talking about marriage until it's a realistic option

Many times a girl will bring up her desires for children, marriage, her house that she wants to decorate and live in, etc., and this can speed up (or shut down) the relationship in an unexpected way. A guy might talk about all his career goals; and about how, some day, he and his wife might want to move to Maine and build a cabin in the woods where they can live off the land. As unromantic as that sounds, it puts extra pressure on making the relationship go to the next level before you have even gotten to know the basics about each other. When it's a realistic option, and you are far along enough in the relationship building, then you can start talking about marriage ideas . . . It's almost always natural. This may come from the guy or the girl at this point. God has used many women to help push forward their dating-to-marriage relationships.

Barbed wire boundary 6: Trying to understand the opposite sex

One thing that every boy knows by the time he is old enough to think is this: he doesn't understand much about girls, but most likely, he likes them a whole lot.

The reality is that even though men don't understand much about women, women don't understand many things about men either. It is easier to see a man's motivation than a woman's, but at the same time, this doesn't mean you understand his motivation in its entirety. If God is leading you into a relationship, it's just good to be educated about the opposite sex so you don't lean on your own understanding (especially if it's based on movies, romance novels, and high school stories). This is why it is healthy to get to know a person *in* relationship before it turns into *a* relationship. It makes the relationship easier and less complicated, but leading into it this way takes a longer process that requires patience. Many people have a get-it-now attitude. If you really want what is best for you, then you will have to trust God and take the normal route. Remember, there are no fast lanes in relationships.

Guys and girls chapters take boundary setting further

I wanted to write even more specifically about some boundaries addressing each of the sexes. Some apply to both, but need to be reinforced with one gender more than another, so read on my little tadpole, read on.

For The Guys

Girls, stop reading. I know you're probably going to read this anyway because girls are so nosy, but you were warned. There is guy talk in this chapter. In all seriousness, though, feel free to read it if you think it will help you, but I'll warn you in advance that it is mildly graphic.

A story

One of my relationships I was in was with a girl who had abstinence in her philosophy of dating. I loved it, except it meant we couldn't kiss until the flower girl marched her petals down the aisle. This was not a deal breaker in the relationship, but I wanted to know why it was so important to her. Well, she needed the commitment because she didn't trust either herself or me because of physical boundaries she had crossed in the past. Despite the fact I would eventually want some innocent lip action when we were on the true road to marriage, I honored her standards because I liked her a lot. (I was even starting to like her in the ways love starts.)

Now, some of you just got offended because I said I wanted to kiss a girl who I was not married to. Each of us has different convictions on this, but let me redeem this a little. Read on.

The #1 reason why breakups happen or suck—people added a physical side to their relationship.

Now that I have gained a little of my credibility back, let's talk reality. I have mentored over a hundred guys and, believe it or not, the ones who were raised in church have the same struggles as the ones who weren't—they just may have had more sexual restrictions than those who haven't had any accountability. Here is what is true, though, of all guys, even if some have had much less experience than the rest of the world: If you press their ON button, then you have started a machine that will only feel complete when the bomb goes off. This is called lust. We all know it; we have all felt it.

The ON button

The problem is each guy's ON lust button is a little, if not completely, different.

- ☐ Some guys get turned ON by a look.
- ☐ Some guys get turned ON by a kiss.
- ☐ Some guys get turned ON by a hug.
- ☐ Some guys get turned ON by kissing.
- ☐ *All* guys get turned ON by giving and receiving more than a few kisses.

Obviously, there are more intentional ways to get the ON button working, but they are obvious ways so we don't need to go there.

When the ON button gets pushed, anything and everything that happens from that point on is like missile command pressing the big irreversible red button—there is no turning back—the interaction will end in your pants and in shame, even if she's not the one to cause the final bomb to go off. The other problem about our ON button is it changes from day to day depending on how good we feel, how our hormones are interacting with our mind that day, or how hot she is (I mean, how spiritual and godly she is . . . yeah that's it . . .), so that means we have a responsibility to set some personal standards so we keep that ON button closed behind a bullet-proof glass box, just like missile command.

Male boundaries in the relationship should be set based on hormones

1. Set physical boundaries based on your own human weaknesses and strengths. Each relationship is different, and just because the last girl's hugs didn't turn you on doesn't mean this girl's won't. Some have just the right way of hugging or the right pressing that will affect you differently. If your ON button starts with the lips, learn to love holding her hand. Special note: Until you are ready to make a commitment, any lip action will lead you down an emotionally-connected road that will push the relationship faster than you want it to go. Some people can kiss without going to the dark place, but everyone will get there if the kisses are just right . . . to stimulate in such a way that, well . . . remember the analogy of the big red ON button?

2. Don't just set your physical standards based on your own strengths and weaknesses; base them on hers too. Did you know one out of four women has been molested, and while 25 percent of women shut down sexually after this, studies show another 50 percent are more willing to cross physical boundaries because of it? This is one example that shows the importance of setting physical boundaries based on both your experience and hers. Get to know/ask her about her experience or lack thereof. Believe it or not, many of the guys I have counseled were not the aggressor when it came to being physical or sexual in the relationship, which leads us to #3 . . .

3. Don't let her state the boundaries in a physical relationship. Many guys will not make the first move, but it is *dangerous* to let your gal

pal dictate what the physical boundaries will be. Many guys will only do what the girl is comfortable with, but when a guy's ON button is pressed, he will follow her down any path she leads. If you are letting a gal pal set the boundaries, she may not even know what she is inviting from you, and it may spiral down to the "uh oh" realm. Let me give you an example. (I have changed the names in this story, so the guy's name is Brick (because most guys are dumb as a brick when hormones are involved). The girl's name is Dolores, which means "causer of pain" (because most women are when it comes to hormones outside of marriage).

Brick and Dolores

Brick was with Dolores for their second outing, and at the end of the date, she began to kiss on his face in a cute way. Then she turned it into even more fun and began to kiss him on the mouth. Brick had never felt this good and had never kissed this long. Then guilt hit him that he felt this good because it was showing (if you don't get that, then don't try). Dolores pressed into the kissing, but Brick, being a good boy, said, "No, wait, we'd better not . . . ," or some other desperate utterance. Then Dolores wanted to help Brick feel good as a man—to help him release some of his sexual frustration. Some things happened (don't use your imagination), and Brick felt awful. He felt like he took advantage of Dolores (he did), but he had never been touched like that before (still don't use your imagination). He came to me for prayer and counsel.

I asked him, "Brick, I know this was new to you, but has she done this before—in other relationships?" He didn't know. We began to pray together, and I had a revelation she had been molested at a young age and, ever since, had been sexually confused about boundaries. She was now enjoying being physical but hating herself for helping her boyfriends out. She had crossed this line a few times. When he went back and asked her, it was very true.

Boundaries based on mutual strengths and weaknesses

You know what awakens the Brick in you the most? It's when you begin a physical relationship without setting boundaries. Without being honest with your weaknesses *and* your partner's weaknesses, you are setting yourself up for failure. As soon as you get past the point of hugs, then it's good to know a little about what you are dealing with in each other. That way, if you are a Brick, then Dolores won't fail with you because you will have grace for her weaknesses and inner-healing journey (and she for your inner-healing journey, if you need one).

Single men are innocent until proven guilty

Let's get back to the main overview for you guys. The religious spirit projected upon many men says you aren't trustworthy and you will fail with a woman just because you are a man. Let me tell you: you are innocent until proven guilty. Your manhood does not have to be a death sentence to you, even with females.

If you have failed you can get back up easily—it just takes work and dedication. Every man has the ability to embrace purity and become super. Shame is one of our worst enemies, and if you live under it, you are going to suffer great limitations. The cross was big enough for all your mistakes to be nailed onto, and they should be left there.

Let me also say, as a father to some and as a brother to others, I have kept everything in my pants, and I've kept all women's hands out of there. I am now in my thirties. You can have this kind of purity, even if you are starting today. Some guys think that because they have already started the lust machine, the only answer to feeding it is to get into a marriage relationship. Not so. God can restore your innocence and, although you will always have a sex drive, you can go back to PG-rated thoughts. I have practiced abstinence, and I know you can too. Maybe it will help some of you to know real purity is available, even as you get older.

So guys, don't be a Brick; define your dating boundaries. Come on, *be a man!* (And girls, if you are reading this, you just made baby Jesus cry . . . ok, ok, maybe not. Maybe this helped you as well.)

The Relationship Flow

The spark hits for someone

They like me too

We go out

They fit my dating skeleton

I keep dating because they fit with my standards & moral compass

We exclusively date for a period of time

We talk about our relationship

We continue to date

We talk about our future

Now you're in the relationship, how is it going to play out? Only God knows, but there is a natural progression you have to begin to look at. When is it time to ask him/her out again? How are you doing at sticking to your standards/compass decisions? To help you map things out, I have your very own handy dandy relationship flow chart.

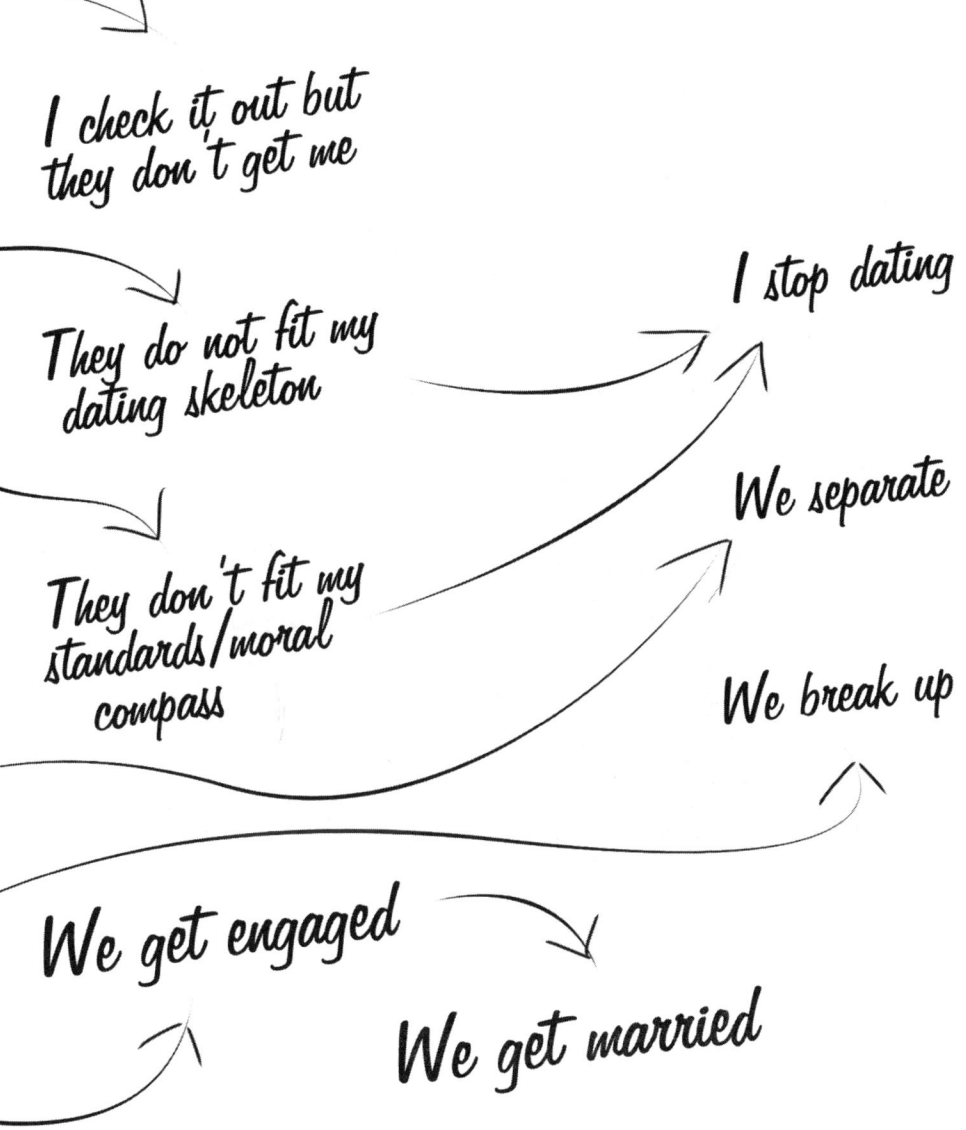

I check it out but
they don't get me

They do not fit my
dating skeleton

They don't fit my
standards/moral
compass

I stop dating

We separate

We break up

We get engaged

We get married

So, assuming your relationship pattern stayed in the column on the left, you are still seeing this person and having a great time. You are following your moral compass. There is no one but each other to tell you when to slow down or speed up. You are going to have to make some of the hardest decisions of your life, but if you exercise balance and work through issues, you will have a great time!

6 Funny Questions to Ask a Date

1. What's your favorite domestic animal? Give me three reasons why.

2. What's your favorite wild animal? Give me three reasons why.

3. If you were deserted on a beach, give me three emotions you'd feel.

4. If you were in a forest, what are three emotions you'd feel?

5. If you were in a white room surrounded by people dressed in white, give me three emotions you'd feel.

6. What's your favorite food? Give me three reasons why.

What's the meaning behind these funny dating questions? What do her answers mean?

1. The reasons she gave for choosing her favorite domestic animal tell you how she thinks other people see her.

2. The reasons she gave for choosing her favorite wild animal tell you how she sees herself.

3. The emotions she gave for choosing how she'd feel on a deserted beach tell you her current views on life.

4. The emotions she gave for choosing how she'd feel in a forest tell you her views on death.

5. The emotions she gave for choosing how she'd feel in a white room tell you her views on marriage.

6. The three reasons for choosing her favorite food tell you her views on sex.

The Fun Side of Dating

Why are romantic comedies so fun to watch, and even more fun to watch if you are with someone significant? Because humanity loves love! We love the idea of sharing ourselves with someone. When we watch other people being romantic, it charges up the best parts of our hopes and dreams. Love makes everything come alive.

Have you ever had the feeling of coming alive inside when someone liked you? Have you ever felt the buzz of excitement from holding the hand of someone you are getting to know? Have you ever felt pain when you had to drop someone at the door and drive away, hoping that your next time to see each other would be the next day? Or how about those who can't stand to be apart, so they have to use their phones 20/7 as a leash for their love?

Getting to know someone of the opposite sex in a romantic way is just plain exciting. There is a buzz in getting to know someone that charges up our hearts to such a degree that nothing else (outside of our relationship with God) can match.

"You complete me."—Jerry McGuire

When we are connecting with someone, it not only meets relational needs, but it also has the potential to complete us. People were created with a hunger and desire for relationships. If one of the most fulfilling and completing kinds of connection is a romantic one, no wonder we swoon when Spiderman gazes at Mary Jane, or when Edward looks into Bella's eyes.

We all have our inhibitions about relationships, but even some of the least likely social candidates for unions seem to be able to find their soul mates. I was speaking at a conference one time which was held in a hotel that was also hosting a *Star Trek* convention. As I walked past Ballroom 4, I discovered it had been transformed into a Redneck Enterprise for the wedding of a Klingon and a Romulin. I was so grateful they found each other, because their *Star Trek* obsession might have been their only chance at true love.

What makes dating fun?

God wants to be fully known by us, and he created the desire for this in us. We want to be known by one person, and to totally know him/her. When we date others and begin to fall in love, we want to know their weaknesses, their strengths, their pain, their life stories, their frames of mind, their emotions, what makes them laugh, what makes them cry, what makes them tick. There is nothing as special as the bond you share with one person that grows tighter as you get to know each other. You begin to "do life" together because you know how to, and it's incredibly fulfilling.

One of the great parts of getting a romantic relationship going is that you start to see how meaningful someone else's life choices affect your own. You learn how to process one person's emotions together, and how to give from the wisdom you have gained already. You learn how to see from someone else's perspective. 1+1 = 2 perspectives—you have teamed up with a perspective on life that doesn't necessarily match your own, but it *does* add depth to it. You grow faster because you allow your heart to be melted and reshaped.

He learned how to dress, she learned how to cook

Life is a discovery process, and when we have two people deliberately discovering life together, we have the potential to draw out a better version of each other. Of course, we also have the potential to hurt each other, but let's focus on why we date, not why we avoid relationships.

Let's think about Mac: He was about to go for the most amazing job interview he had ever had. Before the interview, he stopped to have coffee with his girlfriend, who worked in fashion. She saw how he was dressed and she knew he could look even sharper. She knew how to dress him to impress his interviewers, so she lovingly enhanced him before he went. He got the job, and she got a kiss.

How about Julia, who grew up as a latchkey kid and enjoyed mac and cheese, even into college? She just had no experience with a stove, and the first time she made salad, she thought for sure she should boil it first to get the germs out of it. Yes, she did. She started to date Garvin, who *loved* to cook; he came from an Alabama family who knew how to put southern love into food. He would cook with Julia during their dating time and in doing so, he brought out her inner chef. She now cooks at her family gatherings.

The good thing about getting to know others in a romantic way is that if you keep good boundaries around your heart, you will grow as a person. You will also enable your partners in romance to grow. If you were only in the relationship because you were selfish or shallow, you will only understand your growth needs when you get out of it; but if you really invest yourself, I have no doubt you will grow in your ability to connect in deeper ways.

But she dated a conveyer belt of guys before me!

It's obvious we can have dating baggage, but we can also have a deeper sense of identity after dating others. So some people have over dated or even crossed major lines before in relationships. The choices they make, once those relationships are over, can create a really deep sense of character and identity, especially as God works all things together for His good.

Darla was actually a call girl for four years. She got radically saved at a crusade, and after serving for two years in her church, she began to be pursued by Mark. She didn't feel worthy of his affection because Mark grew up in a strong Christian family. Even after six years of being a Christian, and after working through the issues that caused her to make such bad decisions before she was saved, she felt unworthy because of Mark's caliber.

He also didn't know her story. She was caught between telling him everything and scaring him off, or just outright rejecting him. She talked to her spiritual mom about it. She said, "Girl, you are a new creation in Christ. Let Mark decide if he sees the new creation or the old one. If he doesn't see the new one, he is not worthy of it."

She agreed to go out with Mark. After a few times of just having a blast and getting to know each other, they started to tell their stories. She broke her story to him slowly, but told him the gist of it. He didn't even flinch and responded by saying, "I don't care who you were. I care who you are." They are now happily married with several kids, and you would never know her past because she doesn't wear it anymore. It would make a great movie. Wait! Maybe I should stop writing a dating book and write the next *Pretty Woman*, only the true story version . . . I digress.

The point is: dating is amazing, even if it's hard. It brings out so many relational choices that are essential for us to make in order to become well-rounded people, even if we only ever date the one we end up marrying.

Almost fifty years and counting

I love watching my parents, who have been married for forty-nine years as of this writing. They do so much communicating without ever using words. I watch them cook (they love to cook), and they can manage to use about five words in a half hour as they maneuver around each other in their small kitchen. Sometimes one of them needs something, and they know each other so well that their communication has become almost telepathic. My mom will say, "Here's the salt," and then hand it to my dad before he asks for it.

When you have been together with someone for the long haul, you have the opportunity to know him/her in a way that is spiritual, instinctual, emotional, and physical. It's amazing to see that in society. People like my parents made the commitment to love, and can share a quality of life with each other today that many people in our world will never know. I want that.

Love Letter Madlibs

To a girl from a guy. Fill in the blanks with random words.

1. Noun: _____
2. Body Part: _____
3. Noun: _____
4. A Feeling: _____
5. Type of Profession: _____
6. Noun: _____
7. Place: _____
8. Adjective: _____
9. Body Part: _____
10. Feeling: _____
11. Verb: to _____
12. A Movie: _____
13. Romantic Place: _____
14. Verb: to _____
15. Body Parts: _____
16. Place: _____
17. Feeling: _____
18. Place: _____
19. Silly Affectionate Name: _____
_____

To a guy from a lady. Fill in the blanks with random words.

1. Name of Person: _____
2. Verb: _____ ing
3. Plural Noun: _____
4. Piece of Clothing: _____
5. Noun/Nature: _____
6. Noun: _____
7. Spiritual Gift: _____
8. Verb: _____ ing
9. Body Part: _____
10. Place: _____
11. Weather: _____
12. Verb: to _____
13. Plural Noun: _____
14. Noun: _____
15. Noun: _____
16. Adjective: _____
17. Noun: _____
18. Verb: to _____
19. Noun: _____
20. Adjective: _____
21. Emotion: _____
20. Silly Affectionate Name: _____

From girl to guy
Put the words from the list you filled out into this story.

When you were on the (noun) team I stared at your (body part) today. You looked like a (noun). No one makes me (feeling) the way you do. I am beginning to love you like a (type of person) loves a (noun). When we walk out of the (place), I know people think I am the most (adjective) girl in the world. Just holding your (body part) makes me (feeling). I would love to (action) with you. If I could take you to any movie it would be (movie). After that movie we would bask in/on the (romantic place) and (action) into each others' (body parts). If I were in/on a (place) I would want you with me.

I am so (feeling) to have you in my (place),
(silly affectionate name)

From guy to lady.
Put the words from the list you filled out into this story.

I had a dream about (name of person, hopefully yours) last night. We were (verb) together. There were beautiful (plural noun) all around us. You were dressed in a (piece of clothing). The (noun/nature) made you look like a (noun). I couldn't take my mind off your (spiritual gift). My heart was (verb). We were in/on a (place). The (weather) was (adjective). All we could do was (verb). Moments felt like (plural noun) because I had you in my heart. I had a (noun) for you. I told you if I could, I would give you a (noun). You are the most (adjective) (noun) in my life. I want you to (verb) forever. I love you more than my (noun). I pray we have the most (adjective) relationship together, and I know God is (emotion) about us being together.

Sincerely,
(silly affectionate name)

The "M" Word

God frequently speaks to people who are in a steady relationship. Say you are already dating a special member of the opposite sex and you have invested quality and purity into your times together. Then you hear from Jesus that this is *The One*. Can you trust the voice? More than likely, yes, because you are now praying and listening from a place of realistic safety. You have been keeping your boundaries and honoring the other person, and now your friend and Father is helping to confirm your steps forward.

The reality, though, is that God doesn't want to speak a direct word to everyone about this. **What did Shawn Bolz say? Did he say God doesn't want to speak to me about marriage??**

Communication through His nature

God puts his nature inside us and enjoys our free-choice process of choosing based on that very nature. As you become more mature, you have less of a need to hear direct words from God. The very nature of the One you have been studying in the Bible is gradually coming to life in you. His nature becomes your second nature. When that happens, making decisions is a lot like making decisions in a marriage—the two of you agree together on a course of action. One doesn't wait, cowering in submission, for the other one to give the direct order.

How many married people communicate only through words? Don't they communicate through actions, emotions, facial expressions, and intuitive processes? I talked before about my parents' ability to communicate without the need for words because they have been married for forty-nine years and counting. They know each other's nature, and they can anticipate or read each other. This is a high form of intimate communication. If God always has to speak directly to us, could it be we are acting more like servants than sons? God is not just training us to serve Him; He is training us to partner with Him.

As we grow in the nature of Christ and walk in it, our lives are overcome by His kingdom. God trains us in His nature of love and then releases us into the world to love with His love. This love empowers and gives wisdom to our free choice too. God releases us, His sons and daughters, to make decisions based on the nature of love that has been entrusted to us and placed inside us. God doesn't want to arrange our marriages as much as He wants us to choose love. He wants to partner with us in love. This is understood by the mature, but for those who don't understand God as a father, they just want to get the person who is exactly right for them so they can serve God better. It is such an immature mindset. Thank God it works out sometimes, but that's only because His grace covers so many of our weaknesses.

Let me tell you a story, the story of my friend Pepe (pronounced *Pep-eh.* It's a Latin name I am attached to).

Pepe and his journey into marriage

My friend (name is changed) Pepe was dating an awesome Christian girl. He came from a church background that had taught him if he didn't hear a direct order from God to marry his girlfriend, he would have to break it off. The girl was faithful to Jesus, pure, a leader, and totally dedicated to him. They had an intense talk one night after they had dated for almost a year. She stated her desire for marriage and felt they were ready to pursue engagement, and she wanted to know why he was dragging his feet.

Pepe hadn't heard the voice of God, so he took this as the time to break up with her. He loved her deeply but his theology was faulty. I showed up at the girls' house to visit one of her roommates and was told the sad story. She had cried such a river she'd used up a whole box of Kleenex. I was so mad I drove right over to Pepe's house to kick his butt . . . really. I was mad.

We talked, and I helped him to realize God is a father, not a slave driver. He gives us His nature and then enjoys watching us choose what to do with our desires. We base our choices on the nature of love growing inside us, all the while staying open to a little heavenly help. I told Pepe he really needed to make a manly choice and stop acting like a slave boy who had a leash from a task master around his neck. He wasn't a slave to God's dictatorship; he was a free citizen in a kingdom of love.

I asked Pepe to tell me anything about her he was concerned about, anything that might damage a marriage with her. Although he was in touch with her weaknesses, he couldn't think of a thing that would disqualify her from his heart. He loved the overall picture of this amazing woman. That's when I punched him across the face and called him an idiot . . . No, wait. I imagined that last part. I wanted to punch him, but Pepe realized he was being an idiot. Pepe and the girl got married, and many years later they are still very, very happy and feel they are a perfect match.

Me, personally

I hope I don't hear from God about who I am going to marry until it's time to get into the relationship. Why? Because I love my journey in life, and I don't want it to be consumed with the mystery woman behind Door Number Three whom I have no way of being in a relationship with.

We hear from heaven so we can add depth to our relationship with God and humans. I would love to hear God speak to me when the potential to have a relationship is there, but I almost think it would be even better to just know based on the wholeness God, Himself, is investing in me. That way I can choose based on His desires which are coursing through my veins. What a novel idea—to be one who is so filled with God that I make bona fide decisions.

I do want to become excellent in love, and to work on myself so I can be the fulfillment of someone else's desire. I can control that aspect of the journey. I can spend my time hearing God's voice about how to grow into being the right one, instead of wasting time on a fantasy journey of finding the perfect one for me.

In the end, I believe there is room for people who don't hear directly from God about this, those who hear from God in very clear and powerful ways, and those who make mistakes but then get right back up. The good news is God loves ya. No, really, even when you went on that two-year mission to date that girl who never even knew you existed and then she married the worship leader and you started crying because she forfeited her call to marry the perfect one—you. (I know someone who is reading this who is like that.)

Deception is a lonely road, and it's important to stay balanced.

Not The One;
Breaking Up Well

Facebook posting is a great way to break up: true or false?

When you are in junior high? Oh, so true.

Breaking up is one of the hardest parts of a relationship. What happens when the woman you love is not the woman you are totally in love with? What if, as a woman, you can't fully give your heart to your man?

Good reasons and bad reasons to break up

The good reasons can be handled in a mature way with clear communication. If you dated in a healthy way, you can break up in a healthy way. You don't have to have a one-track goal of just minimizing damage.

Some reasons for a healthy breakup:

- ☐ You realize you don't share the same values.
- ☐ You are not meeting each other's needs.
- ☐ You or your dating partner needs to mature more.
- ☐ You each have radically different goals.
- ☐ There is no true attraction to the other person.
- ☐ The person is not living morally and won't get into a process to change.
- ☐ Your boyfriend admits he snores or has hair on his back, or your girlfriend has every Star Trek book ever written (ok, ok, this one isn't real).

Most breakups hurt more than they should (and cause terrible consequences) for a few reasons:

- ☐ You didn't maintain healthy boundaries in the relationship.
- ☐ You or your dating partner has unprocessed and unresolved pain.
- ☐ You or your dating partner is not mature in communicating.
- ☐ You or your dating partner betrayed trust.
- ☐ Your dating partner doesn't like you as much as you like him/her.

Breakup boundaries/how to successfully walk through the process

Have you ever stayed awake late into the night haunted by pre-breakup anxiety? You have to tell her it's over but you are not sure how. You run through every possible scenario and conversation in your head about one hundred times? You even have imaginary fights for worst-case scenarios so you can prepare your heart? Or you imagine it's all going to be ok when you talk, and you picture the two of you running happily into the sunset together, knowing you are not meant for one another?

People do the most stupid things during breakups. The worst I heard was from a friend whose brother broke off his engagement by text messaging his girlfriend. How did that go, I wonder? Her personalized text messaging ringtone plays, and she happily looks down at her phone screen to see: *Sorry babe, I don't want to marry you. Have a great life! lol*

Another bad breakup I heard about was a story of a young woman who worked at a church. She was one of the pastor's daughters, so everyone knew her and knew about her relationship. She was so nervous about telling her boyfriend it wasn't working that she (irresponsibly) called the staff mass-message line and told everyone it was over because God had told her to get out of the relationship. Her boyfriend was one of the last to hear.

In every aspect of your relationships you should have healthy goals, even goals for the outcome of the end of a relationship. When you decide to break up with someone, you are about to change your life and the life of someone else. Depending on how long you've been dating, this might cause radical change, so how do you do it properly? It's a different answer for everyone, but the first step is to define your breakup boundaries.

1. Define what went wrong and when you discovered it.

This is perhaps the most important information to communicate and be honest with. All people respect truth, but truth has to be conditioned into a package that is appropriate to give. The goal, even in breaking up, is to express love and honor for the person. If you shut that off, then you are allowing yourself to wound him/her. Maybe rehearse to yourself how you would want to hear the truth about your breakup; would you appreciate it if your father told your mother the same way? Would you believe someone if he/she told you the same lines? Breakups don't require hours of talking, they require some definitive, clear communication that can be done in one to thirty minutes.

In defining what isn't working, it could be as simple as Bob's story: Bob wanted to be in business and impact the business world. He felt his purpose in life was to do so. His datee knew her purpose in life was to be a part of long-term mission projects in India. He didn't want to leave the country—even though he valued missions, he wasn't a missionary. She wanted to live forever in India, only coming home from time to time. After being with her for a while, Bob realized this wasn't just a little problem, it was a deal breaker. He had to be honest with her, and when she said she would change and be happy with him, he knew she wouldn't. He stuck to his guns and had a great conversation with her about what she needed, which confirmed he was not her ideal partner for life. They were sad, but it was easily healable.

Then there was the story of Jenny. She was falling in love with a guy who just didn't like her family and friends. He began to isolate her from them, but she loved them too much. After they had an honest talk, he admitted he didn't want to be part of their lives, only hers. She had to be honest and break up with him because her family was part of what she wanted to share with her husband one day.

Your story may be more severe, like Marsha's. She found out the man she loved liked to flirt with her friends. It really offended her, and they had a long talk about it. She told him she wanted to be with someone who respected her boundaries, but she still really cared for him and wished him well. That was one of the best episodes of *Brady Bunch* I ever saw, because it meant Marsha was back on the market for me. I digress.

 Process your heart with someone else before you process it with your date. To go into a breakup talk without processing it first is like being a willing volunteer for an appearance on the *Jerry Springer Show*. You are hoping for the best but expecting the worst.

You were made to be a creature of love and communication, a person who can even process painful things in your heart in a healthy way. Don't process your breakup alone. Friendship is the key to breaking up well. If you followed my advice in another part of this book, you maintained healthy friendships outside your relationship with the other person, so you still have someone to talk to. Don't go e-mailing me because you forgot to keep your friends and now you need help and you are desperate!

I am so grateful I was raised with sisters because they would laugh at my attempts to communicate with girls, but then explain how girls think. This was (and is) so helpful to me because I am a lot less offensive to the female species than I used to be. Women can be equally offensive with their lack of sensitivity to guys. The key is, find out from someone else if what you are going to do, and say, is harsher or softer than it needs to be, and don't go in without getting your heart and mind equipped.

2. Communication is everything, so choose your words wisely

Processing your breakup talk will take the sting out of the rejection. It will help you to be clear, gentle, and wise. One of the hardest things to do is to communicate everything with words that are easily understood, or to use healthy and upfront communication. The best breakups lead the datees into a place where there does not have to be any, if just a little, follow up. The worst breakups make you feel as if things are still unresolved and you want to talk some more each time you think about the person.

So how do you do this? Do you get in front of the mirror like Theo on *The Cosby Show*? Only if you want the same results as him: a woman scorned. (Popquiz: Who can guess which episode I am talking about? My apologies to the readers for all the *Nick at Night* references.) Use this opportunity to learn how to communicate. Set some goals for your talk to ensure you don't use words that lead the person on further. If you are breaking up, then communicate that with no hope attached. The worst thing you can do is say something like a girl did to my friend:

I really like you . . . no, I really do! It's just I'm in a time of finding myself, and maybe something will work out later but I'm just not ready for a serious relationship right now, but I really, really like you . . .

So my friend was in love with her all the way up until her marriage . . . and it wasn't to him. That's when he realized she hadn't been honest.

3. Assess how you will act when you still share mutual friends & social space

One of the main goals you should have, when processing your breakup with her, should be to define what the breakup might mean for everyone else. Answer these questions to yourself in advance:

- ☐ Do you work together? How are you going to act around each other?
- ☐ Do you share friends in your friendship networks? How are you going to respond to their questions?
- ☐ Are you at church together? How will you both handle that?

Most couples break up and find each side wants to completely distance him/her self from the other, but this is selfish and immature unless the relationship was abusive. You don't have to be best friends with the other person, or even more than acquaintances, but you can't be manipulative and cut him/her out of your life (or vice versa). This is not a divorce unless you had unhealthy boundaries in the first place. You should be able to move on, even while still having to see him/her. It's called dying to yourself and pushing past the pain.

Many times if you date others, their hearts open up in a big way. Then you break up with them and they date someone else very soon after your breakup because they are getting ready for marriage. Are they on the rebound?

What if they date someone from your mutual friendship pool? Is that unreasonable or is that real? The key is to release them, get released from them, and then hope and pray for the best. They might prosper in finding someone else before you do. Are you going to be ok with that? Can you let them make their own choices and be mature about them?

The preparation breakups bring

Many couples break up, but both parties should have developed a genuine friendship during their dating relationship. Sometimes this friendship lives on, but painfully; sometimes it can't because of the mixture of attractions and emotions. The great thing about breakups is that if you were able to invest in the dating relationship in a healthy way, you will have learned how to train yourself when in new relationships. That means it wasn't all for nothing, and your ability to maintain great boundaries and standards with one person will translate beautifully into friendships and relationships with others.

It's always good to evaluate yourself about one month after you break up. Give yourself a checkup and feel around for lumps . . . in your heart. You will find that if you continue to allow God to work on you, when you talk to Him about your relationships and process them with Him, you will see how He is training you to love. That journey can be painful, but you may find as you grow older that the pain you experience is just growing pain.

I think the most precious thing Christians can do when they break up with others is use *releasing* language with them. "I release you, and I give you back everything you gave me so you can give it to the right person." This may make the other people uncomfortable, but it is vital to not just give others an emotionally clean break, but a spiritual release also.

And Now . . .

The Conclusion

The End.

Ok, ok, there is more to it than The End . . .

Now that we've reached the end of the book, I think the most important thing I could say to you is:

Have fun!

Think of all the amazing couples you know—the ones that are legit and the ones that are portrayed in the media. You are supposed to feel like you can have an even better relationship than theirs. It's not a competition, but it is an invitation to learn from the best and worst of what's happened in the marriages of your parents, your friends, celebrities, and even presidents. Position yourself for an epic romance.

The Huxtables were an amazing couple in the 80's, but their show is done. Romeo and Juliet were in love many centuries ago and they went and killed themselves . . . not too happy an ending there. JZ and Beyoncé are a power couple, but they may or may not have a powerful relationship behind closed doors. Prince Charles and Princess Diana fought for something they later ended with a piece of paper. Homer and Marge may have been married for twenty-plus years, but they are only cartoons! You are real, and your relationship has the potential to be your absolute favorite example of a stellar marriage (it should be at the end of the day)!

Relationships are supposed to be a source of life, so if you get into one, enjoy the pursuit! I also want you to know that these thirty-plus years of being single have not been bad for me at all. I have thoroughly enjoyed my days and years so far. Being single is a worthy lifestyle. Some of you need to try it!

I hope this guide has challenged you into thinking differently about your current and future relationships. I hope you have decided to set deliberate standards and boundaries for them. I also trust that this guide has helped

you to define your own journey in life, and that you have determined
to be as healthy and balanced as possible—spiritually, physically, and
emotionally.

I challenge you as you continue on your journey with this truth: When
single or in a relationship, you can have balance, intentional relationships,
healthy processing, and a clear road map for what you choose to walk into.
I pray God guides you forward every step of the way.

I also remind you that, as a Christian, the needs you have can be met.
Jesus assured this. He paid the most incredible price so you could be free
to have life and have life abundantly! You are now available for the best!

Lastly: *You are in charge of the relationships you build, so be empowered!* No
one can do for you what you have the amazing ability to do for yourself.

Signing off,

Shawn Bolz

Your Offical
I'm Ready to Date Badge

This badge is proof
that I am an amazing catch
and am thoroughly prepared
for a successful relationship.

Just cut it out and wear it to the next social activity for singles. They will know that by reading this book, you have thoroughly prepared yourself for a real relationship. Wearing it will ensure that you meet someone special!

(Money-back guarantee not offered in all states.)

Dating Quotes

"When I was in high school, I got in trouble with my girlfriend's dad. He said, 'I want my daughter back by 8:15.' I said, 'The middle of August? Cool!'" —*Steven Wright*

"Computer dating is fine, if you're a computer." —*Rita Mae Brown*

"Employees make the best dates. You don't have to pick them up and they're always tax-deductible." —*Andy Warhol*

"I was on a date with this really hot model. Well, it wasn't really a date date. We just ate dinner and saw a movie. Then the plane landed." —*Dave Attell*

"I was dating a guy for a while because he told me he had an incurable disease. I didn't realize it was stupidity." —*Gracie Hart*

"Odds on meeting a single man: 1 in 23; a cute, single man: 1 in 429; a cute, single, smart man, 1 in 3,245,873; when you look your best, 1 in a billion." —*Lorna Adler*

"I want a man who is kind and understanding. Is that too much to ask of a millionaire?" —*Zsa Zsa Gabor*

"Dating is so insecure. My last relationship, I was always there for her and she dumped me. I told her about it. I said, 'Remember when your grandma died? I was there. Remember when you flunked out of school? I was there. Remember   when you lost your job? I was there!' She said, 'I know—you're bad luck!'" —*Tom Arnold*

"An archeologist is the best husband any woman can have: the older she gets, the more interested he is in her." —*Agatha Christie*

"Women marry men hoping they will change. Men marry women hoping they will not. So each is inevitably disappointed." —*Albert Einstein*

"Put your hand on a hot stove for a minute and it seems like an hour. Sit with a pretty girl for an hour and it seems like a minute. That's relativity." —*Albert Einstein*

"You know it's love when you want to keep holding hands even after you're sweaty." —*Anonymous*

"A man is already halfway in love with any woman who listens to him." —*Brendan Francis*

"Love is an electric blanket with somebody else in control of the switch." —*Cathy Carlyle*

"The trouble with some women is that they get all excited about nothing—and then marry him." —*Cher*

"When we got married I told my wife, 'If you leave me, I'm going with you.' And she never did." —*James Fineous McBride*

"You have to walk carefully in the beginning of love; the running across fields into your lover's arms can only come later when you're sure they won't laugh if   you trip." —*Jonathan Carroll*

"No matter how lovesick a woman is, she shouldn't take the first pill that comes along." —*Joyce Brothers*

"The bravest thing that men do is love women." —*Mort Sahl*

"Love is blind—marriage is the eye-opener." —*Pauline Thomason*

"I know that somewhere in the universe exists my perfect soulmate—but looking for her is much more difficult than just staying at home and ordering another pizza." —*Alf Whit*

"If love is blind, why is lingerie so popular?" —*Unknown*

"Love is temporary insanity curable by marriage." —*Ambrose Bierce*

"A man is incomplete until he is married. After that, he is finished." —*Zsa Zsa Gabor*

"The most happy marriage I can picture would be the union of a deaf man to a blind woman." —*Coleridge*

"Whatever you may look like, marry a man your own age—as your beauty fades, so will his eyesight." —*Phyllis Diller*

"Love at first sight is possible, but it pays to take a second look." —*Unknown*

"When I was a young man I vowed never to marry until I found the ideal woman. Well, I found her, but alas, she was waiting for the ideal man." —*Unknown*

"Love is like the measles; we all have to go through it." —*Jerome K. Jerome*

"Love is like any other luxury. You have no right to it unless you can afford it." —*Anthony Trollope*

More Bad Pickup Lines

You make me melt like hot fudge on a sundae.

Pick up a pack of sugar that actually says sugar on it and say, "You dropped your nametag!"

What does it feel like to be the most beautiful girl in this room?

Are your legs tired, because you've been running through my mind all day long?

Do you have a Band-Aid? Because I just scraped my knee falling for you.

There must be something wrong with my eyes; I can't take them off you.

Girl, you'd better have a license, cuz you are driving me crazy!

I hope you know CPR, because you take my breath away.

I must be in heaven, because I'm standing next to you!

If I could rearrange the alphabet, I'd put U and I together.

You must be from outer space cuz I can see the stars in your eyes.

Hi, I'm Mr. Right. Someone said you were looking for me.

Do you believe in love at first sight, or should I walk by again?

Do you have a map? Because I keep getting lost in your eyes!

Is there an airport nearby or is that my heart taking off?

Apart from being sexy, what do you do for a living?

Are you accepting applications for your fan club?

Are you an interior decorator? When I saw you the room became beautiful.

Are you going to kiss me or do I have to lie to my diary?

Are you lost, ma'am? Because heaven's a long way from here.

Are you Natasha, my contact?

Have you been praying much? Good, because I'm the answer to your prayers.

Baby, if you were words on a page, you'd be what they call fine print.

Baby, somebody better call God, cuz He's missing an angel!

Baby, you must be a broom, cuz you just swept me off my feet.

Baby, you're so sweet, you put Hershey's outta business.

Can I get a picture of you so I can show Santa what I want for Christmas?

Come live in my heart and pay no rent.

Compared to you, the sun feels cold.

Did the sun come out or did you just smile at me?

Do you have a sunburn, baby, or are you always this hot?

Do you know karate? Cuz your body is really kickin'.

Don't walk into that building—the sprinklers might go off!

Don't you know me from somewhere?

Excuse me, but I may be lost . . . Can you give me directions to wherever you're going?

Excuse me; I think you have something in your eye. Nope, it's just a sparkle.

For a moment I thought I had died and gone to heaven. Now I see that I am very much alive, and heaven has been brought to me.

God must have been in a very good mood today, because I met you.

Have you always been this cute, or did you have to work at it?

Have you been eating Cocoa Puffs? Cuz I'm goin' coko for you.

Hey, kitten, how about spending some of your nine lives with me?

Hey, I need your help! My mom says that if I don't get a date by tomorrow, she's putting me up for adoption.

I didn't know that angels could fly so low!

I didn't know that Miss America lived here!

I think I feel like Richard Gere—I'm standing next to you, the Pretty Woman.

I'd marry your cat to get in the family.

If a star fell for every time I thought of you, the sky would be empty.

If beauty were a grain of sand, you'd be a million beaches.

If beauty were sunlight, you'd shine from a million light-years away.

If beauty were time, you'd be an eternity.

If I could reach out and hold a star for every time you've made me smile, I'd hold the sky in the palm of my hand.

If I had a rose for every time I thought of you, I would be walking through my garden forever.

If water were beauty, you'd be the ocean.

If you were a laser, you'd be set on stunning.

If you were a library book, I would check you out.

If you were a new hamburger at McDonald's, you would be a McGorgeous.

I'm looking for a friend . . . do you want to be my friend?

About the Author

Shawn Bolz is the senior director/pastor of Expression58 in Los Angeles, California—a Christian ministry and humanitarian aid organization. Formally a partner of WhiteDove Ministries and a founding member of the International House of Prayer–Kansas City, Shawn speaks across the globe on various Christian subjects, dating now added to his repertoire. He is also a well-known television and radio host, and has worked with God TV, the Miracle Channel, and TBN, to name a few. His heart is to see Christians activated, living out their purposes, and loving the less-fortunate people of the world in practical ways.

Expression58
11271 Ventura Blvd. #500
Studio City, CA 91604

www.expression58.org
office@expression58.org

Resources from Shawn Bolz

The Throne Room Company

Thought provoking and profoundly perceptive, *The Throne Room Company* has the power to revolutionize your understanding of God. In this book, Shawn Bolz reveals a fascinating message from heaven that will penetrate the deep places of your heart. His stories and wisdom will guide you to a nobler place.

SHAWN BOLZ

Keys

TO

HEAVEN'S
ECONOMY

AN ANGELIC
VISITATION
FROM THE
MINISTER
OF FINANCE

Foreword by JOHN PAUL JACKSON

Keys to Heaven's Economy

Heavenly resources have only one purpose—that Jesus Christ would receive His full reward and inheritance in our age. Just as God held nothing back from Solomon, who longed to build a tabernacle for God on earth, God will hold nothing back from a generation of people who long to bring Jesus everything that belongs to Him! God is about to release finances and resources to reshape the Body of Christ on the earth. God is looking for those who desire an open-door experience with the One who is the master of all keys—Jesus.